The Reed
Concise Māori
DICTIONARY

Te Papakupu Rāpopoto a Reed

The Reed
Concise Māori
DICTIONARY

Te Papakupu Rāpopoto a Reed

Māori – English • English – Māori

Sixth Edition (Revised)

Compiled by A.W. Reed
Revised by Tīmoti Kāretu
This edition revised by Ross Calman

REED

REED PUBLISHING (NZ) LTD
TE KARUHI TĀ TĀPUI O REED (AOTEAROA)

Established in 1907, Reed is New Zealand's largest
book publisher, with over 600 titles in print.

www.reed.co.nz

Published by Reed Books, a division of Reed Publishing (NZ) Ltd,
39 Rawene Rd, Birkenhead, Auckland. Associated companies, branches
and representatives throughout the world.

ISBN-13: 978 0 7900 0777 9
ISBN-10: 0 7900 0777 0

© 1948, 1984, 2001 Literary Productions Ltd, T.S. Kāretu, Ross Calman

First published 1948
Reprinted 1949
Second edition (New Zealand and Great Britain) 1951
Reprinted 1956, 1958, 1960
Third edition (revised) 1962
Reprinted 1964, 1968
Fourth edition (revised) 1971
Reprinted 1973, 1974, 1978
Fifth edition (revised) 1984
Reprinted 1985, 1987, 1988, 1989, 1991, 1992, 1998
This edition (revised) 2001
Reprinted 2003, 2004, 2005

Printed in New Zealand

Contents

Preface to 2001 Revised Edition

Tēna rā koutou katoa. This latest edition of the *Reed Concise Māori Dictionary* includes many new and revised entries which reflect common usuage at the beginning of the twenty-first century.

In a dictionary of this type it is not possible to list all specialist terms, or go into all the subtleties of meaning of the Māori language. *Te Matatiki Contemporary Māori Words*, published by Te Taura Whiri i te Reo Māori, is an invaluable guide in the area of new technologies, sport, fashion and other areas. The H.M. Ngata *English–Māori Dictionary* is also recommended as it includes many modern usages absent from earlier dictionaries, is comprehensive, and provides example sentences. As always, the H.W. Williams *Dictionary of the Māori Language* remains the authority on vowel length and the root meanings of words and is recommended to the serious scholar of the Māori language.

In recognition of the preference in Māori for the passive voice, passive terminations are included in this edition. They appear with many common words in the Māori–English section of the dictionary, e.g. kite, to see, becomes the passive kitea, to be seen, with the addition of an a; this appears thus: kite(-a). These are a guide only, as preference for passive endings varies from region to region (see Tīmoti Kāretu's comments in his preface).

Transliterations that are established in the Māori language are no longer specifically marked, although in most cases their provenance will be readily apparent.

As noted by Tīmoti Kāretu, a word in Māori can serve many grammatical functions. Where there might be ambiguity, the part of speech is marked by use of the articles 'the' or 'a', or the preposition 'to', to indicate whether it is a noun or a verb, e.g.

rebel, a tutū.
rebel, to whana.

Shades of meaning which depend on context are indicated within parentheses, e.g.

sentence (grammar) rerenga; (prison) whiu.

It is not practicable to include all regional variations but some of the more common ones have been included in this edition, e.g. 'ētahi' and 'ētehi', 'hea' and 'whea'.

Themed vocabulary lists, which previously appeared in the body of the dictionary, can now be found at the end.

The Māori language is a great taonga, bequeathed to our present generations by those who have gone before. Learning any language takes time and hard work, but one's efforts are rewarded by attaining insights into a unique worldview. My hope is that users of this dictionary will fall under the spell of the language and wish to immerse themselves ever deeper in all its richness and depth.

Ūkuikui ai ki te hoāka.

Persistence pays off.

Ross Calman
Ōtautahi, 2000

Preface to 1984 Revised Edition

When first approached to work on the revision of this dictionary, I was a little reluctant because it meant criticising and correcting someone else's efforts. However, this initial reluctance was overcome by my greater desire to have as accurate as possible a dictionary which would be of use to the person who is not a scholar of the Māori language but merely wants a quick reference to certain words, their meaning and use.

The dictionary does not purport to be the final authority on the language, and the reader should be aware that there are many words not included which are nevertheless used in different tribal areas. Included, however, are a number of words not used in everyday conversation which will smack of quaintness to many native speakers! But words considered to be too obsolete, archaic or regional have been omitted from this edition.

A.W. Reed stated in his introduction to earlier editions that 'no attempt has been made to give an extended selection of modern words added to the Māori language, for there would be no ending to the task.' Many transliterations were included, though, and indicated accordingly with an asterisk. In a number of instances, paraphrasing rather than transliterating has been employed by speakers of the language. Further examples of both ways of providing Māori equivalents for English words are now included here.

Generally the active form of the verb has been listed; for example, 'kite' — 'to see' will be found rather than 'kitea' — 'to be seen'. The passive voice is preferred to the active in spoken Māori, so some familiarity with the passive terminations (-a, -hia, -ia, -ina, -kia, -mia, -na, -nga, -ngia, -ria, -ta) is strongly recommended. Another fact to be noted is that a word in Māori can serve many grammatical functions, e.g.

mahi	to work (verb)
te mahi	work (noun)
tangata mahi	working man (adjective)

The causative prefix 'whaka-' is added to many words, thus 'whakamahi' — 'to set to work'. To simplify matters such words will be found listed alphabetically under 'WH' in this dictionary.

Since the dictionary only provides a list of words and their equivalents in Māori or English, it can only be a guide. To be able to use the words with accuracy, the dictionary should be used in conjunction with a good grammar and a more detailed dictionary such as H.W. Williams's *A Dictionary of the Māori Language* (Government Printer). Occasionally the Māori language contains no simple equivalent to English words. The English verbs 'be' and 'have', for example, cannot be translated by one word in Māori, and detailed grammatical explanations would be necessary to convey the Māori modes of expression in such cases. Such explanations are outside the scope and purpose of this dictionary, and to avoid complexity and confusion for all but the most serious students of Māori culture. These too fall outside the scope of this work.

Another important improvement in this edition concerns the use of macrons. They are essential in differentiating between the meanings of words, as well as giving an indication of pronunciation and stress. For example, there is a great deal of difference between the following words:

kaka	clothing
kakā	alight, i.e. on fire
kākā	parrot

or	keke	cake
	kekē	creak
	kēkē	armpit

There was a tendency in previous editions to list all words spelt the same way — but with different vowel lengths — under the same heading. This practice has been discontinued, and indeed it will be noticed that macrons have been applied consistently throughout the dictionary to encourage better understanding and greater accuracy in pronunciation.

Prior to this edition there was a remarkable lack of essential and common words such as:

whare paku,
whare iti   toilet, lavatory

Also words describing certain parts of the anatomy and their functions, absent from previous editions, have now been included.

It is hoped that these alterations will make this dictionary more interesting, useful and worthwhile.

He tao rākau e taea te karo
He tao kī e kore e taea te karo!

A wooden shaft can be parried,
Not so a verbal one!

T.S. Kāretu
University of Waikato, 1983

Pronunciation

The ten consonants in Māori are:

h, **k**, **m**, **n**, **p**, **r**, **t**, **w**, **ng**, **wh**.

The first eight are generally pronounced as in English, with some refinement for the **p**, **r** and **t**. The **p** and the **t** should be somewhat softened so that the **p** can sound closer to a **b** and the **t** more like a **d**, especially when it comes before **a**, **e**, or **o**. With the **r**, the tongue should tap the back of the front teeth similar to the pronunciation of the **d** or **l** in English. The last two are digraphs, **ng** being pronounced as the **ng** in singer, **wh** as **wh** in whale, or as **f**.

The five vowels are:
a, **e**, **i**, **o**, **u**.

They are pronounced in two ways: short and long.
Long vowels are indicated by a macron, e.g. **ārai**, in which the first **a** is long. Diphthongs are elided, e.g. **ai** (ah-ee) is sounded as **i** in high.

Māori – English

A

ā, a and; as far as; the … of (ngā … ā) forming the possessive (plural); until; when. (This word has many uses which cannot be detailed here. As a preposition it means 'of', 'at', 'at the time of', 'after the manner of', etc, and as an adverb 'well'.)

ā iwi national.

ā kōruā your (plural, addressed to two people).

ā koutou your (plural, addressed to three or more people).

ā mātou our (plural, their and my).

ā māua our (plural, his or her, and my).

ā mua from now on.

ā rātou their (plural, addressed to three or more people).

ā rāua their (plural, two people).

ā rohe local, regional.

ā tahirā the day after tomorrow.

ā tātou our (plural, addressed to three or more people).

ā tāua our (plural, your and my).

āe agree, yes.

aewa unhealthy.

aha anything at all; do what to?; what?

ahakoa although; while; whether.

ahau I; me.

āhea? when? (future time).

āhei able, possible; collarbone.

ahi fire.

ahi kā home fires; retain ownership through occupation.

ahiahi afternoon; evening.

Ahitereiria Australia.

aho fishing line; string.

ahu care for; heap; move towards or point in a certain direction.

āhua appearance, character, form, make; quite; way.

āhua mate unhealthy.

āhua ngākau mood.

āhuaatua rude.

ahuahu care for; heap.

āhuareka pleasant; pleased.

āhuatanga characteristic; way.

ahunga direction; generation.

ahurei unique.

ahurewa altar.

āhuru comfortable.

ahuwhenua agriculture; agricultural; industrious.

ai has many uses in Māori, some of them not capable of exact translation: regularly, habitually; there is; used as substitute for relative pronouns; refers to action and events; to copulate; sexual intercourse.

ai! oh!

āianei now, soon, today.

aihe dolphin.

aihikirīmi icecream.

aikiha handkerchief.

aikiha pepa tissue.

āio calm.

aitanga copulation; descendants.

aituā ill-omen; misfortune, accident.

aka vine; rātā vine, *Metrosideros albiflora* and *M. perforata*.

aka wāina grapevine.

akatea white-flowered rātā vine, *Metrosideros albiflora* and *M. perforata*.

ākau shore, coast (especially rocky); bank (river); reef.

ake very; own; self; a word having intensifying force; from below, upwards; indicates continuation of time; indicates degree.

ake, ake, ake for ever and ever.

akeake tree, *Dodonaea viscosa*.

ākengokengo tomorrow.

akepiro shrub, *Olearia furfuracea*.

āki(-na) to dash.

akiaki urge, incite; red-billed gull, *Larus novaehollandiae*.

akiraho shrub, *Olearia paniculata*.

ākiri(-tia) throw away.

ako(-na) learn.

ākonga learner, student; disciple.

akoranga learning; lesson.

āku my (plural).

aku my (plural).

ākuanei soon.

ākuara a little while.

Ākuhata August.

akutō late.

āmai giddy.

āmaimai nervous.

amakura red-tailed tropic bird, *Phaethon rubricauda*.

Amerika America.

āmine amen.

āmiomio giddy; revolve.

amo(-hia) carry; litter; stretcher.

amokapua chief; priest.

amokura red-tailed tropic bird, *Phaethon rubricauda*.

amorangi leader; priest.

āmua time to come.

amuamu complain; grumble.

āmuri after, later.

āmuri ake nei hereafter; later.

āna her, his (plural); yes.

anā there.

ana cave; when; the phrase 'e … ana' with verb denotes continuance of action.

anahera angel.

anāianei from this time onwards.

anake only, without exception; alone.

anamata hereafter.

ananā! indeed!, an interjection expressing admiration.

ānao certainly.

ānau wander.

anei here.

ānewa to reel; fall; weak; listless.
ānewanewa giddy.
aniana onion.
ānini giddy; headache.
aniroro giddy, light-headed.
āniwaniwa rainbow.
ānō as if, as though.
anō again; also; exactly; indicates admiration; own (with a possessive pronoun); self (with a pronoun); yet; still.
anu cold (noun); spit.
anuanu disgusting; disgusted.
anuhe caterpillar, larva of sphinx moth *Agrius convolvuli*.
anga shell, skeleton; framework.
angaanga chief; elder; head.
angamate back.
anganui to face towards.
āngi fragrance
angi free; freely.
angiangi free; diaphanous.
ao bright; cloud; dawn; daytime; world.
ao hurihuri the modern world.
ao mārama the world of life and light; this world.
ao tawhito the world of our ancestors.
ao tukupū universe.
ao tūroa the light of day; this world.
aoake the day before; the day after.
aoake nui two days off.
aoake nui atu three days off.
aoakewake several days off.
aoināke the next day.
Aotearoa New Zealand.
apa slave.
apakura song of lament.

āpānoa until.
apārangi crowd; group of distinguished people; party of workers or slaves.
apataki retinue.
Āperira April.
āpiha officer.
āpiti add; attack; bewitch; friend; gorge, pass; to supplement; to place together.
apo to gather together; to grasp; to extort; to heap up.
apoapo entangle.
āpōpō tomorrow; sometime.
āporo apple.
apu gather; gust; working party.
apuapu gobble.
arā and then; namely; in other words; that is; interjection of surprise.
ara(-hia) awake; to rise; path, road, way.
araara trevally, *Pseudocaranx dentex*.
arahanga bridge; ladder.
araheke stairs.
ārahi(-na) guide; lead.
ārai(-a) keep off; screen; barricade; apron; curtain.
aramaiangi escalator.
ārani orange (fruit).
Aranga Easter.
aranga become famous.
arapoka tunnel.
ararā! over there!
arata lettuce.
arataki(-na) to guide; to lead.
ārau entangle; entangled.
arawhata bridge; ladder; stairs.
are open; overhanging, concave.
are! what!
arearenga hollow.

arero tongue; tongue or striking point of taiaha.

arewhana elephant.

āria deep water.

ariā concept, idea, notion, theory; effect, impact; feel (noun), feeling (noun); resemblance; visible emblem or representation of an atua.

ariā hirahira special effects.

ariki chief; chiefly, noble; first-born in notable family.

ārita eager.

aro desire; front; mind (noun).

aroākapa front rank, row.

aroaro face; front.

aroaro o, i te in the presence of.

aroaroā lonely.

aroaromahana spring (season).

aroha(-ina) love, affection; compassion, pity.

ārohi examine; look for.

aronga direction.

arotahi focus, take aim; lens; contact lens.

aru follow.

aruaru interrupt.

aruhe edible fern-root, root of *Pteridium aquilinum* var. *esculentum*.

ātā expression of disgust.

āta carefully; gently; slowly.

ata form, shape; morning; early morning.

ata hāpara dawn.

ata marama moonlight.

ata mārie good morning.

ātaahua beautiful; pleasant.

ātae how great.

atamira platform.

ātārangi shadow.

atarau moon; moonlight.

atarua bad eyesight.

atawhai friendly; be kind to; to long for.

atawhai kino unfriendly.

ate liver.

ātea free; clear; cautious.

ātea tūārangi outer space.

ateate bosom; calf of leg.

atewharowharo lungs.

āti descendant; hence tribal prefix as in Te Āti Awa.

atu other; very; a word having the force of a comparative or superlative; indicates motion onwards; away.

atua ghost; god.

āu your, yours (plural).

au I, me; current, wake of a canoe; whirlpool; gall; howl.

au o te moana, te open sea.

aua far away; far on; not; those (already mentioned); yelloweye mullet, *Aldrichetta forsteri*.

aua ake I do not know.

aua atu never mind.

aua hoki! I have no idea!

auahi smoke.

auarā certainly there is (in reply to a negative question).

auau often; bark; howl.

auē groan; to lament; alas!, oh no!.

auaha leap.

auināke tomorrow.

aukaha lashings.

aukume magnet.

auporo strike (industrial action).

aurere groan, despair.

auru break off; destroy.

autaha to one side.

autāne brother-in-law (of a woman).

auwahine sister-in-law (of a man).

awa river, stream; channel; furrow, valley.

awaawa valley; groove.

āwake two days off.

āwakewake four days off.

awakeri drain.

āwangawanga distress; disturbed; undecided; worried.

awatea broad daylight; noon.

awe cloud; soot.

āwhā rain; storm.

awhe gather into a heap; surround.

āwhea? when? (future time).

Awherika Africa.

āwheto vegetable caterpillar; a large caterpillar, larva of sphinx moth *Agrius convolvuli.*

awhi(-tia) embrace; cherish; draw near to.

āwhina(-tia) help.

āwhiowhio whirlpool; whirlwind.

E

e o (vocative case); indicates a number; in the phrase 'e ... ana' with verb denotes continuance of action; (preceding verb) imperative; (following passive verb) by; if; of course; when.

e ai ki according to.

e hē! no!, that's wrong!

e hia? how many?

e hoa form of address, friend.

e hoa mā form of address, friends.

e kī! e kī! expresses disagreement.

e kō form of address, girl.

e kore e taea impossible.

e noho rā farewell (said by those leaving).

e tika! e tika! well, well!

e whia? how many?

ea to be avenged; to be paid.

ehara absolutely not.

ehara i te hanga! it is no ordinary thing! (exclamation of surprise or admiration).

ēhea? which? (plural).

ehi! well!

ehu to bail.

eka acre.

eke(-a,-ngia) to board, to climb onto something, to mount, to get into a car or other form of transport; to place oneself on something or someone else; to ground, to land; to achieve, to reach.

ēnā those (nearby).

ēnei these.

engari but, but rather; it is better; on the contrary.

engia expresses agreement.

epa to pelt, to throw at.

epeepe distant relations.

ērā those (far off).

erangi but (after negative).

ētahi several; some.

ētahi wā sometimes.

ētehi several; some.

etia as if; how great!; perhaps.

eweewe blood relation.

ēwhea? which? (plural).

H

hā breath; flavour, taste; so; then; what!

hae(-a) to cut up; to tear.

haeana iron.

haeata beam of light; dawn.

haeatatanga opening through which light shines.

haemata cut up uncooked food.

haere to go, to travel; journey.

haere mai come here; welcome!

haere rā farewell (said by those remaining behind).

hāereere stroll; travel about.

haerenga trip, journey.

haerenga pokanoa joyride.

hāhā catch the breath; leaning; seek; shout at.

hahake naked.

hāhau seek.

hāhi church, religion, denomination.

hāhū to disinter bones of dead.

hāhunga tūpāpaku exhumation of dead.

hai as; at; for; to; with; preposition indicating future time; forms the imperative; not.

haina sign.

hainatanga signature; signing.

hāka jar.

haka war-like chant with actions.

hakahaka low.

hākari entertainment; feast; gift.

hākawa fool.

hake hunchback; hockey.

hakeke fungus.

hākerekere crowd; hair cut short.

haki flag; cheque.

hakihaki itch; covered with sores.

Hakihea December.

hākinakina fun; sport.

hakiri to be felt, or heard indistinctly.

hākirikiri vague.

hako ugly; clown.

hākoakoa brown skua, *Catharacta skua.*

hākoro father; old man.

hākorukoru wrinkle.

haku chief; complain; grumble; weep openly; yellowtail kingfish, *Seriola lalandi.*

hama hammer.

hāmama open; shout; vacant.

hāmamamama yawn.

hāmanu ammunition.

hamarara umbrella.

hāmaremare slight cough.

hāmeme grumble; mutter.

hāmipēka hamburger.

hamo back of head.

Hāmoa Samoa.

hāmoemoe sleepy.

hāmua elder brother; elder sister.

hamumu speak.

hāmumumumu mutter.

Hana Kōkō Santa Claus.

hanaweiti hundredweight.

hanawiti sandwich.

hāneanea comfortable; lounge suite.

hanehane decay.

Hānuere January.
hanga (passive **hangā, hangaia**)
  build; make; mend; pour out;
  group of people.
hāngai relevant; across (at right
  angles); opposite.
hangarau technology; joke.
hangatītī tease.
hāngi earth oven in which food
  is cooked by hot stones;
  contents of the oven.
hao enclose; greedy,
  acquisitive; catch fish using a
  net.
haona horn.
hāora hour; oxygen.
hapa absent; error, mistake;
  pass over; supper.
hāpai(-tia) advance guard;
  carry; lift up.
hāpaki catch lice.
hāpara dawn.
hāparangi shout, bawl.
hape crooked.
hāpiapia sticky.
hapori family; section of tribe.
hapū clan, sub-tribe; pregnant.
hapui betrothed, engaged.
hāpuku groper, *Polyprion
  oxygeneios.*
hara to miss; offence; sin; to
  violate tapu.
harakeke New Zealand flax,
  Phormium tenax.
harakore innocent (not guilty).
haramai come, arrive.
harapaki steep slope.
hararei holiday.
Haratua May.
hārau graze.
harawene envy, jealousy.
hari(-a) carry; joy; pleased;
  rejoice.

hari koa glad, pleased,
  overjoyed.
harirū shake hands and press
  noses.
harore mushroom.
haruru dull sound; roar.
hātakēhi hard-case.
Hātarei Saturday.
hāte shirt.
hātea faded.
hātepe cut off.
hau air, wind; breath; essence;
  famous; seek; vitality, vital
  essence; strike.
hau ārai ozone layer.
hau kāinga home.
hauā crippled; lame.
hauaitu pass out; perished with
  cold.
hauata accident.
hauāuru west; west wind.
hauhake(-a) dig up, harvest;
  take up.
haukū dew, damp.
haukoti intercept; an
  intercepting body of warriors.
haumāuiui result of work.
hāunga besides, except for,
  with the exception of.
haunga offensive smell;
  stinking.
hauora health; healthy; fresh
  air.
haupaoro golf.
haupapa ambush.
haura invalid.
haurangi furious; mad;
  drunken.
hauraro north; north wind.
haurua half.
haurutu dew.
hautai sponge.
hautoki intercept, surround.

hauwhā quarter.
hawa broken.
hāwhe half.
hāwini servant.
hē wrong; fail.
he a, some.
he aha? what?
he aha ai? why?
hea what place?; any place.
heahea silly.
hei as; at; for; to; with; preposition indicating future time; forms the imperative; hay.
hei aha never mind.
hei aha? what for?
hei konā goodbye (on telephone)
hei konei rā farewell (said by those leaving).
hei tā according to.
heihei fowl; noise.
heitiki greenstone neck ornament.
heke descend; migrate; rafter.
hekenga migration.
hekerangi parachute.
hekeretari secretary.
heketā hectare.
heketaunga descent of hill.
heketoro fairy.
hēki egg.
hēko sago.
hemo died; disappear; to be faint; pass away.
hengahenga girl.
hengia black skin.
hēneti cent.
hēnimita centimetre.
heoi however.
heoi anō denotes completion of statement.
heoti however.

hepapa zebra.
hēpara shepherd.
Hepetema September.
hēra sail.
hēramana sailor.
here guide; tie; tie up.
herehere prisoner, slave; captivity.
hereni shilling.
Hereturikōkā August.
heru comb.
hetiheti hedgehog.
heu choked with weeds; eaves; pull apart; razor; to shave; to clear undergrowth.
heuea be separated.
heuheu scatter.
hī(-a) to fish with hook and line; raise up.
hia how many?; passive termination.
hiahia to want; long for, yearn for.
hiainu thirst; thirsty.
hiakai hunger, hungry; appetite.
hiako skin.
hiamoe sleepy.
hīanga naughty.
hiawai thirst; thirsty.
hihi stitchbird, *Notiomystis cincta*; ray of sun.
hihi kōkiri x-ray.
hihiani radar.
hihiko active; quick.
hihiri industrious; long for.
hika daughter; form of address; girl; kindle fire by friction.
hika! goodness me!
hikahika chafe; rub.
hīkaikai wiggle.
hikareti cigarette.
hīkari calf of leg.
hīkaro extract.

hiki(-tia) carry in arms; hold; lift; raise.
hikihiki to nurse.
hikipene sixpence.
hiko to shine; electric; electricity; flash of lightning.
hīkoi to walk, march.
hiku end, rear; tail of a fish or reptile.
hikutau head of valley; source of river.
hīmene hymn.
himu hip.
hina grey hair.
hīnaki eel pot.
hinapōuri sad; very dark.
hinātore glow; twinkle.
hīnau tree, *Elaeocarpus dentatus*.
hine daughter; girl.
hinenga girlhood.
hinengaro desire; heart; conscience; mind.
hinu oil, fat, hence anything of similar consistency, e.g. lard, dripping, petrol, hair oil, etc.
hinga defeated, died; fall; to lean; slant.
hingareti singlet.
hiore tail (of a four-legged animal).
hipi sheep; ship.
hipohipo hippopotamus.
hīpoki(-na) to cover; covering.
hira abundant; multitude; important.
hiranga excellent; excellence; importance, significance.
hīrangi heatwave.
hīrawhe giraffe.
hīrere to rush; shower; waterfall.
hirihiri repeat charms.

hiripa slipper.
hiriwa silver.
hītako yawn.
hītekiteki tiptoe.
hīti sheet.
hītimi marble; marbles.
hītoki hop
hītoko hop
hītori history.
hiwa watchful.
hiwi to jerk a fishing line; line of descent; ridge.
hoa friend; husband; wife; partner; ally.
hoa rangatira partner, spouse.
hoa tāne husband, male partner.
hoa wahine female partner, wife.
hoahoa diagram, figure.
hōanga sandstone used for cutting and grinding weapons.
hoangangare enemy.
hoari sword.
hoariri enemy.
hoatata neighbour.
hoatu give.
hoawhawhai enemy.
hoe(-a) oar; paddle; to row; to paddle.
hoehoe to paddle canoe.
hoetere upstart.
hōhā boring; bored; fed up; nuisance; wearisome.
hōhipera hospital.
hōhonu deep.
hohoro quick.
hohou rongo make peace.
hoi deaf; distant.
hōia soldier.
hōiho horse.
hoiho yellow-eyed penguin, *Megadyptes antipodes*.

hoihoi noisy.
hoihoi! be quiet!
hokai extended.
hokarari ling, *Genypterus blacodes*.
hoki also; and; because; for (as conjunction); return; used to express emphasis.
hōkioi a fabulous bird, supposed never to have been seen.
hoko (prefix) twenty times, e.g. hokorua = forty.
hoko(-na) buy; sell; barter; lover.
hoko ki tai export.
hoko ki uta import.
hokoitinga childhood.
hokomaha supermarket.
hokomirimiri to pat; to stroke.
hokowhitu company of warriors (literally 140).
homai give (to the speaker).
hongere channel (TV).
hongi press nose in greeting; to smell.
honi honey.
hono crowd; retinue; join.
honohono continual.
hononga connection; link; network; relationship; union.
hōnore honour.
honu deep; turtle.
honu whenua tortoise.
Hōngongoi July.
hōpa sofa.
hōpane saucepan.
hōpara belly; thorax.
hope the main body of an army; waist.
hopi soap.
hopi makawe shampoo.
hopohopo fearful.

hopu(-kia) catch; catch up; record (audio).
hopu ataata video recorder.
hōpua pond; pool.
hopuoro microphone.
hopureo tape deck.
hora(-hia) scatter; spread out.
hore bare, bald; not.
hore rawa not at all.
hori mistake; tell lies, prevaricate.
hōro hall.
horo(-a) fall in pieces; landslide; to slip down; stormed; to swallow; taken.
horoeka lancewood, *Pseudopanax crassifolius*.
horohoro remove tapu.
horoi(-a) wash.
horokaka ice plant, *Disphyma australe*.
horomi(-a) to swallow.
horopaki context.
horopito pepper-tree, *Pseudowintera axillaris* and *P. colorata*.
hororē vacuum cleaner.
horowhenua avalanche, landslide.
horu yell.
hōrua toboggan.
hōtēra hotel.
hōtoke cold; winter.
hotu long for; sigh; sob.
hou new; modern; fresh; enter; bind.
houhere industrious; lacebark, *Hoheria populnea*; mountain ribbonwoods, *H. glabrata* and *H. lyallii*.
houhou unpleasant.
houtete stunted.
hū hiss; quiet; silent; boot; shoe.

hua egg; fruit; product; result; abound; abundant.

hua hīmoemoe grapefruit.

huahua game, especially birds preserved in their own fat; sketch, draw.

huarākau fruit.

huawhenua vegetable.

huaki(-na) attack; to open; uncover.

huamata salad.

huanui road.

huānga relative; member of same hapū.

huanga advantage, benefit.

huangō asthma; short of breath.

hūāpapa flat rocks.

huarahi highway, road; way.

hūare saliva.

huarite rhyme.

huata spear.

huatahi eldest child; only child.

huatau polite.

huatea childless.

hūhā thigh.

hūhi discomfiture.

huhu grub, larva of beetle *Prionoplus reticularis*; strip off covering; waste away.

huhua numerous, many.

hūhuna barbecue; grumbling.

hui meeting, gathering, assembly; to meet.

huia extinct bird, *Heteralocha acutirostris*; feathers of huia; valued treasure.

huihuinga meeting, gathering, assembly.

huinga group, set.

hūiki suffering from cold; half-frozen.

huirua two at a time.

Huitanguru February.

huka cold; foam; frost; snow; sugar; icing; last man killed in battle.

hukahuka foam.

hukapapa frost; ice.

hukarere snow.

huke dig up.

hukinga head of valley; source of river.

huku hook.

hūmārie beautiful, peaceful.

hūmārire beautiful, peaceful.

hume to taper.

humuhumu stripped of main parts.

huna(-ia) to hide; kill, destroy.

huna kanohi mask.

hunahuna concealed.

hunaonga daughter-in-law; son-in-law.

hunarei father-in-law; mother-in-law.

hunarere father-in-law; mother-in-law.

Hune June.

hunōnga daughter-in-law; son-in-law.

hūnua high, infertile country.

hunuhunu scorched.

hunga group of people.

hunga kore mahi the unemployed.

hunga pāpāho the media.

hungarei father-in-law; mother-in-law.

hungawai father-in-law; mother-in-law.

hūngoingoi old woman.

hupa soup.

hūpana fly back; fly up.

hūpeke bend; draw up arms or legs; jump; old woman.

hura remove; uncover.

hura kōhatu unveiling (of a headstone)

Hūrae July.

huri(-hia) go; turn; change; overwhelm; grind.

huri noa right around.

hurihau windmill.

hurihuri reflect upon; turn over; tumble drier.

hurikaikamo eyelash.

huripara wheelbarrow.

huripoki furrow.

huritau anniversary; birthday.

hūrokuroku continuously; jogging.

huru glow; hair; feather.

huruhuru bristles; coarse hair.

huti (passive **hūtia**) pull up.

hūtu suit.

hutukawa head-dress of red feathers.

hutupōro football.

hūwai cockle, *Chione stutchburyi*.

hūware saliva.

I

i indicates the past tense; as a preposition it connects a transitive verb with its object; along; at; while.

i te mea because.

ia current; each; every; he; her; him; it; she; that.

iaia sinews; veins.

ianā then.

iarā! indeed!

iāri yard.

iaua! here!

ihi power, essential force; coward.

ihiihi exciting, stirring; shudder; terrified.

iho essence; downwards; from above; heart; lock of hair; ordinary; tohunga or principal person in a crew of canoe; unimportant; umbilical cord.

ihu bow of canoe; nose.

ihu oneone good worker (literally, ihu = nose, oneone = earth, meaning 'dirty face').

ihumanea clever.

ika fish; troop; victim; warrior, especially the first one to be killed in battle.

ika a Whiro veteran.

ikarangi galaxy.

ike high.

ina for, since, when; conjunction; has the effect of emphasising (often with emphasis on the a, inā).

inahea when (of the past).

ināia tonu nei right now.

ināianei now, soon, today.

ināianei tonu right now.

inaina warm yourself.

inake recently.

inaki waka traffic jam.

inakuanei just now.

inakuarā recently.

inamata formerly; immediately.

inanahi yesterday.

īnanga whitebait *Galaxias maculatus*; shrub *Dracophyllum longifolium*.

inangeto in a little while.

inaoake two days ago.

inaoakenui three days ago.

inapō last night.

inatahirā two days ago.

inawhai not long ago.

inawheke not long ago.

ine(-a) measure; gauge, meter.

ine taumaha weigh.

inei? is that so?

īnihi inch.

inihua insure; insurance.

iniki ink.

īnoi(-a) beg; pray; prayer; request.

inu drink.

inuinu sip.

Ingarangi England.

Ingarihi English.

ingoa name.

ingoa kārangaranga nickname.

ingoa whānau surname.

io lock of hair; muscle; nerve.

ioio muscular, good stature (of males); stubborn.

ipo darling; lover; pet.

ipu calabash with narrow mouth; container; vessel; bottle.

ipurangi toadstool; internet.

irā! there!

ira freckle; mole.

ira atua of supernatural beings.

ira rukeruke radioactive.

ira tangata human life.

iraira freckle.

irāmutu nephew; niece.

iri(-a) to be hanging; rest upon.

iriiri baptise.

iro maggot.

iroiro vermin.

iroriki germ.

ita held firm.

itahirā the day before yesterday.

iti small; minimum.

itiiti tiny.

ito enemy.

iwa nine.

iwi bone; nation; tribe; people; strength.

iwi whānui the public.

iwituararo backbone.

K

kā(-ngia) light (verb); to be alight, burning.

ka introduces a new action or condition; when.

ka pai! good!

kāeo shellfish.

kaha strong; strength; ability; persistency; line of descent; rope, lashing; file of men in war party.

kahakaha garment.

kāhaki(-na) carry away, kidnap; hijack.

kahakoretanga weakness.

kaharoa seine net or large drag net.

kahawai fish, *Arripis trutta*.

kāheru spade.

kahika ancestor; chief.

kahikatea white pine, *Dacrycarpus dacrydioides*.

kāhiwahiwa very dark.

kāhō batten.

kāhore no; not.

kāhu Australasian harrier (hawk), *Circus approximans*.

kāhu korako old harrier with light plumage, used figuratively for a chief.

kahu garment; cloak (there are many descriptive names of garments beginning with kahu, e.g. kahu-kererū = cloak covered with pigeon feathers, kahu-tāniko = cloak of fine flax with an ornamental border, etc); stillborn baby; chief.

kahu moe pyjamas.

kahu tangatanga dressing gown.

kāhui cluster; flock.

kahunga slave.

kahupapa to cover with staging.

kahurangi treasure, precious item; dame; blue.

kai(-nga) eat; food products; to have full play; as a prefix it means a body of persons engaged in work, or the agent who performs the work denoted by the verb, e.g. whakamāori = to translate or interpret; kaiwhakamāori = translator, interpreter (see also kei).

kai inati overdose.

kai paipa to smoke (cigarettes etc).

kai roro quiz.

kaiā steal; thief.

kaiahuwhenua farmer.

kaiaka adept; adult; man.

kaiaka-mīhini mechanic.

kaiākiko wounded man.

kaiako teacher.

kaiamo mēra postie.

kaiārahi leader, guide.

kaiauru vandal.

kaihanga creator; builder.

kaihautū captain, leader.

kāihe donkey (jackass).

kaihī fisher.

kaihoro eat greedily.

kaihou lover.

kaihua tree on which birds are speared.

kaiiwi strange people.

kaikā eager; impatient.
kaikaha keen.
kaikamo eye.
kaikanikani dancer.
kaikiri dislike.
kaikōhuru murderer.
kaikōmako tree, *Pennantia corymbosa*.
kaikora lazy person.
kaikōrero speaker.
kaikuti makawe hairdresser.
kaimahi worker, employee.
kaimanga vegetarian.
kaimātai whatu optician.
kaimoana seafood.
kāinga village; country; home; house; address.
kainga a word which indicates the scope of work.
kainga kanohi view.
kaingākau to value.
kaioma runner.
kaiotaota vegetarian.
kaipakihi business; business person.
kaipara athlete; athletics.
kaipatu ahi firefighter.
kaipōkai tūārangi astronaut.
kaiponu refuse to let go; selfish; greedy.
kaipuke ship.
kaipūtaiao scientist.
kairapu hara detective.
kaireperepe relation by marriage.
kairīpoata journalist.
kairoro lover.
kairuku diver.
kairuri surveyor.
kaitā giant, huge; large.
kaitaka fine cloak with ornamental border; whipping-top.

kaitapere actor; actress.
kaitaraiwa pahi bus driver.
kaitiaki guardian; trustee; caretaker; babysitter.
kaitiakitanga guardianship.
kaitiora pirate.
kaitirotiro inspector.
kaitoa brave man; warrior; serves you right!
kaitohutohu coach (sports); director (film).
kaituhi writer.
kaitukumahi employer.
kaituku miraka milkman.
kaiurungi pilot.
kaiwaewae messenger.
kaiwaiata singer.
kaiwawao referee, umpire.
kaiwhaiwhai fan (admirer).
kaiwhakaahua photographer.
kaiwhakaatu model (fashion).
kaiwhakahaere director, manager, leader.
kaiwhakataetae athlete; competitor.
kaiwhakatangitangi musician.
kaiwhakatuma terrorist.
kaiwhakawā judge.
kākā native parrot, *Nestor meridionalis*.
kaka hair; fibre; ridge.
kaka o te ihu bridge of nose.
kaka rēhia tracksuit.
kākahi chief; freshwater shellfish.
kākahu(-ria) clothes; to dress; garment.
kākahu ōrite uniform.
kākāiti budgie.
kakama quick; active.
kākano berry; seed.
kakanga slave.
kakapa flutter; throb.

kākāpō ground parrot, *Strigops habroptilus*.

kakara flavour; smell (pleasant).

kākarauri to be dusk; hardly seen.

kākāriki red-crowned parakeet, *Cyanoramphus novaezelandiae*; yellow-crowned parakeet, *C. auriceps*; green.

kakati sting.

kakau handle.

kakawa sweat.

kake(-a) ascent; climb up; overcome.

kakī neck; throat; black stilt, *Himantopus novaezealandiae*.

kama eager.

kāmahi tree, *Weinmannia racemosa*.

kāmaka rock (noun).

kāmera camera.

kāmera ataata video camera.

kāmera tere speed camera.

kamonga eyelash.

kamupene company, business.

kāmura carpenter.

kanae grey mullet, *Mugil cephalus*.

kanapa bright.

kānapanapa gleaming; dark green.

kānape no; not.

kanapu bright.

kānara candle.

kanekane garlic.

kānekeneke move about; from place to place.

kānewha unripe, immature; underdone; doze.

kani to saw; a saw.

kanikani dance.

kāniwha barbed spear.

kano seed; colour; sort, kind.

kanohi eye; face.

kanohi ki te kanohi face to face.

kānuka tree, *Kunzea ericoides*.

kānga corn.

kānga papā popcorn.

kānga pirau rotten corn.

kānga wai rotten corn.

kanga abuse; curse.

kangaru kangaroo.

kāo no (in reply to a question).

kao cooked and dried kūmara.

kaokao ribs; armpit; side.

kāore no; not.

kāore he tangata nobody, no one.

kāore anō not yet.

kāore kau not at all.

kaoriki little bittern, *Ixobrychus minutus* (extinct).

kapa a row; team; copper.

kapahaka Māori performing arts group; Māori performing arts.

kapakapa wing; flutter.

kāpata cupboard.

kāpata kākahu wardrobe.

kape eyebrow; to refuse.

kapekape stick used to rake out embers, poker.

kāpene captain.

kāpeti cabbage.

kapi covered; occupied.

kāpia kauri gum; glue.

kapiti gorge, pass; crevice; shut in.

kāpō blind.

kapo(-hia) snatch; flash; lightning.

kapowai dragon-fly.

kapu palm of hand; sole of foot; cup.

kapua cloud.

kāpui to lace (shoes).
kāpura fire.
kara colour; flag.
karaehe class (school); glass.
karaihe grass.
Karaitiana Christian.
karaka New Zealand laurel, *Corynocarpus laevigatus*, and its berry; orange; clerk; clock; o'clock.
karakahia grey duck, *Anas superciliosa*.
karekare surf, waves.
karakia incantation; spell; prayer, worship (modern usage).
karāmu gram.
karamū shrub, *Coprosma* species.
karamuimui swarm.
karanga(-hia,-tia) call; call out in welcome; hail; to term.
kārangaranga call frequently.
karangatanga relationship; relative; occupation; category, class.
karapoi around; surround; to be surrounded.
karapu club, society.
kararehe animal; dog.
kararehe kōwao wild animal.
karari toy, 'jumping jack'.
karate karate.
karāti garage.
karauna crown; the Crown, government.
karawaka measles.
karawhiu(-a) whirl around, thrash around; debate; 'give it heaps'.
kāre not.
kare dear, darling; heater; stove; ripple.

kareao creeper, supplejack, *Ripogonum scandens*.
kārearea New Zealand falcon or bush hawk, *Falco novaeseelandiae*.
kare-ā-roto emotions.
kare-a-roto sweetheart.
karehā the day before yesterday; the day after tomorrow.
karekare surf, waves.
karekō calico.
kareparāoa cauliflower.
karēpe grape.
karēpe tauraki raisin.
karere messenger; message.
karere hiko email.
karetao toy, 'jumping jack'; puppet; robot.
kāreti college; carrot.
kāretu sweet-scented grass.
kārewa to launch; melt; buoy; float; surface of water.
kāri card, postcard; garden.
kāri moni money card.
kāri nama credit card.
kari(-a) dig.
karia by and by.
karihi stone (of fruit); tooth; nuclear.
karihi-kau nuclear-free.
kāriki garlic.
kariri cartridge; ammunition.
karo(-hia) to parry, fend off; avoid; soon.
karokaro slave.
karoro black-backed gull, seagull, *Larus dominicanus*.
karu eye; head.
karu whakarahi microscope.
kāruhiruhi pied shag, *Phalacrocorax varius*.
karukaru glaring; rags; torn clothes.

karupango pupil (of eye).
kata(-ina) laugh.
kāta cart.
kātae! how great!
kātahi then; expresses appreciation.
kātahi anō just now; only just.
katare stoop.
katau right hand, right-hand side.
kātete leg.
katete size.
kāti finish; that's enough.
kati(-a) bite; close; shut.
katikati bite frequently; to move the jaws.
kātipa constable.
katipō venomous spider, *Latrodectus katipo*; wasp.
kato flowing; flood (of tide).
katoa all; altogether; completely; every; whole; wholly.
Katorika Catholic.
kātua adult; full-grown.
kau ancestor; alone; as soon as; bare; cow; empty; in vain; only; pupil (of eye); swim.
kaua no; do not; should not.
kauae beam; chin; jaw.
kauaemua eldest brother; eldest sister.
kauaeraro youngest child; terrestrial lore.
kauaerunga celestial lore.
kauahi lower piece of wood used in making fire by friction.
kauaka do not.
kauati chief; important person.
kauhau lecture; preach; recite; speech.
kauhoe swim.

kauhou line of descent.
kaui shoelace; cord.
kauika school of fish; pod of whales; heap.
kaukau bathe, swim; anoint.
kaukauranga bathing place; bathroom.
kaumātua elder; elderly; old (person); old man; old woman; adult.
kaunihera council.
kaunoti pointed rubbing stick used in fire-making.
kaupane head.
kaupapa cause; fleet of canoes; floor; level surface; platform; principle; project; purpose; subject, theme, topic.
kaupapa here policy.
kauraka do not.
kauranga ford; swim (noun).
kauri tree, *Agathis australis*; soot from burnt kauri gum, used for tattooing.
kaurimarima rubbing stick, used in kindling fire by friction.
kāuru head of tree; head of river.
kāuta cooking-shed; kitchen.
kautāhanga empty.
kautangatanga moving quickly.
kaute account; count; bill.
kaute pēke bank account.
kauwae beam; chin; jaw.
kauwaeraro youngest child; terrestrial lore.
kauwaerunga celestial lore.
kauwhau lecture; preach; recite; speech.
kawa charmed; disliking food; acid; sour; bitter; protocol.
kāwai line of descent.

kawaka tree, New Zealand arbor vitae, *Libocedrus plumosa.*

kawakawa pepper-tree, *Macropiper excelsum.*

kāwana governor.

kāwanatanga government.

kawau black shag, *Phalacrocorax carbo.*

kawau-paka little shag, *Phalacrocorax melanoleucos brevirostris.*

kawe(-a) bring; carry; strap.

kawe rongo headphones.

kāwei line of descent.

kaweka line of descent (indirect).

kawenga responsibility.

kawititanga o te ringaringa wrist.

kawiu scalp; dried.

kāwhaki(-na) take by force; kidnap; hijack.

kāwhe calf (young cow).

kawhe coffee.

kāwhena coffin.

kē different; other; otherwise; step- (e.g. tungāne kē, or tungāne kēkē = step-brother); strange; afterwards; before; already.

kea mountain parrot, *Nestor notabilis*; false; lie.

kēhi suitcase.

kehokeho clearly.

kēhua ghost; spirit.

kei as; at; in; in the act of; lest; like; on; stern (noun); while; with; used in place of the verb 'to be' in its many forms.

kei hea? where?

kei mua in front.

kei muri behind.

kei te pai it's okay, fine.

kei whea? where?

keiwhā before; while.

kēkē armpit.

keke cake.

kēkeke embrace.

kekeno seal (animal), *Arctocephalus forsteri* and sea-lion, *A. hookeri.*

kēmihi chemist.

kemokemo wink; blink.

kēmu game; match.

kēna wai watering can.

kenakena Adam's apple.

kenepuru silt.

keo peak.

keokeonga top or peak of hill.

kerei grey.

kerēme claim.

kerepe grape.

kerepeti pottery.

kerepō blind.

kererū New Zealand or wood pigeon, *Hemiphaga novaeseelandiae.*

keri(-a) dig.

kete basket; kit; handbag.

kī(-a) full; key; to say; to term.

ki at; against; for; into; if; on; to; towards; with; connects verb with object.

kī nāianei up to the present time.

kia let, indicating something that is to happen; wish or purpose.

kia kaha be strong.

kia ora hello, welcome, thank you; literally 'good health'.

kia tūpato be careful.

kīaka calabash.

kīano not yet (used of the past).

kiato assembled.
kiekie shrub used in weaving, *Freycinetia banksii.*
kīhai not (in the past).
kihi indistinct (sound); kiss.
kihikihi cicada, *Melampsalter cingulata, M. muta*; kiss.
kīhini kitchen.
kikī crowded; tight; full.
kīkiki idiot; mad.
kikikiki stutter.
kikimo eyes tightly closed.
kiko flesh; body.
kikokiko of flesh and blood.
kikorangi blue sky; blue.
kikowhiti forearm.
kimi(-hia) look for; seek.
kimo to wink.
kina sea urchin, *Evechinus* species.
kīnaki relish (noun).
kini pinch.
kino bad; evil; to dislike; hurriedly; to ill-treat; ugly; damaged; harm; injury.
kino ake worse.
kīngi king.
kiokio fern, *Blechnum capense.*
kiore rat; mouse.
kiri bark (tree); skin.
kiri angaanaga scalp.
kiri kā fever.
kiri kau naked.
Kirihimete Christmas.
kirihou plastic.
kirikau leather.
kirikiri basket; gravel.
kirikiti cricket (sport).
kirimana agreement, contract.
kirimate chief mourners, close kin of deceased.
kirīmi cream.
kirimoko tattooed skin.

kiripaepae receptionist.
kiripaka flint; quartz.
kiritaki customer.
kiritapu single (unmarried).
kiritata neighbour.
kiritea fair (of complexion).
kiritona pimple; mole; wart.
kiriwai skin.
kiriwara drug addict.
kiriweti unpopular.
kirokarāmu kilogram.
kiromita kilometre.
kita fast; tightly.
kite(-a) discover; find; recognise; see; sight, vision.
kitemea if.
kiwa wink.
kiwi brown kiwi, *Apteryx australis.*
kiwi-pukupuku little spotted kiwi, *Apteryx owenii.*
kō digging implement, sometimes used as a weapon; dig or plant with a kō; yonder place; a distant time; sing (as birds); at; to; form of address to a girl.
kō atu the futher side.
kō mai the near side.
koa happy, pleased; indeed; please.
koakoa stupid.
kōanga spring (the season for planting).
koara koala.
kōaro upside down.
koata quarter.
kōataata transparent.
kōauau flute played with nose or mouth.
koe you (singular).
koekoeā long-tailed cuckoo, *Eudynamis taitensis.*

koha(-ina) gift; respect.
kōhaia girl.
kohake father; old man.
kōhamo back of head.
kōhanga nest.
kōhanga reo Māori language pre-school.
kōhatu stone; pebble.
kohe talk nonsense.
kohekohe New Zealand cedar, *Dysoxylum spectabile.*
kōhī skeleton; young man.
kohi(-a) collect, gather; tuberculosis.
kōhia New Zealand passion vine, *Tetrapathea tetrandra.*
kohikohinga collection.
kōhimuhimu whisper.
kōhine girl.
kōhinu petrol.
kohinga collection.
Kohitātea January.
kohitū tuberculosis.
kōhoi thin.
kōhonihoni nibble.
kohu mist, fog; concave; hollow.
kōhua to boil; pot (for boiling water, etc).
kōhūhū tree, *Pittosporum tenuifolium.*
kohukohu hollow.
kohuku unfinished.
kōhumuhumu whisper, murmur; short hair.
kōhungahunga child.
kōhuru ill-treat; murder; treachery.
kohutapu New Zealand shore plover, *Thinornis novaeseelandiae.*
kōhutuhutu tree fuchsia, *Fuchsia excorticata.*

koi sharp, spike; headland; lest, in case; while.
koia that's it, that's right; indeed; gives emphasis to a question.
koinā that is, those are; like that.
koinei this is, these are; like this.
kōingo(-tia) yearn.
koirā that is, those are; like that.
kōipuipu footsore.
koitareke New Zealand quail, *Coturnix novaezealandiae.*
kōiti little finger; little toe.
kōiwi bone; corpse; descendants (plural); fellow (used as an expression of contempt); person; self; skeleton.
kōkā mother; aunt.
kōkako blue-wattled crow, *Callaeas cinerea wilsoni*; orange-wattled crow, *C. cinerea cinerea.*
koki angle; corner (of a road, path, etc).
kōkiri advocate, push for; leatherjacket (fish), *Parika scaber*; throw; thrust.
kōkō tūī, *Prosthemadera novaeseelandiae*; cut in tattooing.
koko scoop; shovel; spoon; corner (of a room, house, etc).
koko tātaki witty speaker.
kokoiti teaspoon.
kokonga corner.
kokopi close; shut.
kōkopu freshwater fishes of *Galaxias* species.

kokora natural (as opposed to foster) mother.
kokotaha tablespoon.
kokoti ambush; cut across; intercept.
kōkōwai red ochre; earth from which red ochre is obtained.
kōmā pale.
koma gram.
kōmata nipple.
kōmeke pounded fernroot.
komekome chew; grumble.
komiti committee.
komo put in.
kōmore bracelet.
kōmukumuku to scrub.
komuri backwards.
kōmutu surprise.
konā that place; that time.
konei this place; this time.
kōneke sledge.
koneke slide along; rollerblades; rollerskating.
konihi stealthy.
kōnini tree fuchsia, *Fuchsia excorticata*, or fruit of tree fuchsia.
konohete concert.
kōnohi grieve; yearn.
kōnui thumb; unit of measurement (length of first joint of thumb); big toe.
kongakonga crumb; fragment.
konganuku metal.
kongangi creek.
kongene withered; wrinkled.
kōngenge exhausted.
kōngutu mouth of river.
kōpā numb, stiff; congealed, set; cramped, confined.
kopa bag used for expressing oil from berries; disappear; crippled; satchel; sandal; schoolbag; wallet.
kōpae circular; lying side on; disk (computer); hemisphere.
kōpae puoro record (noun, music)
kōpaepae puoro compact disk.
kōpaki covering; gift to dead person; to wrap; envelope.
kōpako back of the head.
kōpani(-a) lid; to shut.
kōpapa small canoe; surfboard.
kōpara bellbird.
kopareti skates.
kope sanitary pad; nappy.
kōpere arrow; bow; dart; sling; rainbow.
kōpeti loop; snare.
kopi full stop.
kōpiha pit for catching rats.
kōpiko meander.
kōpikopiko wandering; winding.
kōpiro intestines; putrid, rotten.
kōporo van.
kōpū belly; calf of leg; womb.
kōpua deep (water).
kōpūpū blister.
kōpura seed kūmara, potatoes, etc.
kōputa blistered.
korā that place (distant).
kora fragment; spark.
koraha open country; desert; mud-flats; shallow.
kōrako albino.
kōrakorako fairies.
kōrangaranga ache.
kōrapa cage.
kōrapu flash; shine.
kōrari flower-stem of flax, *Phormium tenax*.

kōrau wild turnip.
kore no; not; will not; nothing, zero.
kore mahi unemployed.
kōrea wheelchair.
koreke New Zealand quail, *Coturnix novaezealandiae* (extinct).
kōrenga broken place.
kōrengarenga crushed; overflowing.
kōrere small channel; gutter; pipe; spout; diarrhoea.
kōrero(-hia,-tia) conversation, discussion; news; quotation; say; speak; story; talk.
kōrero ahiahi idle stories.
kōrero pūrākau folk-tale; story; legend.
kōrero tara folk-tales.
kōrerorero discuss; talk a lot.
koretake useless.
kōreti kayak.
kori move; wriggle.
kōriha gorilla.
korihi sing (of birds).
korikori move; wriggle.
korikori tinana exercise.
korimako bellbird, *Anthornis melanura.*
korirangi cloak decorated with black and white thrums of unscraped flax.
koro old man; grandad, grandpa (form of address); father; noose.
kōroa finger; forefinger.
koroahu steam.
koroheke old man.
koroiti little finger; little toe.
korokē extraordinary; fellow (used as expression of contempt).

korokio shrub, *Corokia* species.
korokoro throat; finger; toe; loose.
koromahanga loop; noose.
koromatua thumb; big toe.
koromiko shrub, *Hebe salicifolia, H. stricta* etc.
koropeke limbs doubled up.
koropiko bow down; kneel.
koropuku hidden; swollen.
koropungapunga porous; decayed; pumice.
koropupū boil; bubble up.
kororā blue penguin, *Eudyptula minor.*
kōrori stir.
korōria glory.
korotū skull.
koroua old man; grandfather.
korowai cloak ornamented with black twisted thrums.
korōwha golf.
korowhāwhā anchovy, *Engraulis australis.*
korowhio to whistle.
koru folded; shrub, *Pratia physalloides.*
kōrua you two.
kōruarua hole; pit.
korukoru wrinkle.
kōrure mottled petrel or rainbird, *Pterodroma inexpectata.*
kota cockle-shell; lime; sawdust.
kotahi one (not used by itself, but in this form: kotahi rau = one hundred).
kotahitanga unity.
kotakota chips, shavings.
kōtamu keep opening and shutting lips.

kōtare sacred or New Zealand kingfisher, *Halcyon sancta vagans*.

kotere swelling.

koti coat.

kotiate small flat weapon of wood or bone with lobed blade.

kotikara finger; fingernail; toe; toenail.

kotikoti cut to pieces; divide lands among the hapū; to decide on boundaries; striped.

kotinga division; boundary line.

kōtingotingo speckled.

kotipū cut off.

kotiri meteor.

kōtiritiri meteor.

kōtiro girl.

kotiti be distorted or displaced; move aside.

kōtītiti wander about.

kotiuru headache.

kōtiwhatiwha here and there.

kōtore anus; younger brother (used in genealogies).

kōtuhi smog.

kōtui zip.

kōtuitui network.

kōtuku white heron, *Egretta alba*.

kōtuku-ngutupapa royal spoonbill, *Platalea regia*.

kōtukutuku tree fuchsia, *Fuchsia excorticata*.

kōuma breast-bone.

kōura crayfish, *Jasus lalandei* and *Paranephrops planifrons*.

koura gold.

koutou you (plural, three or more people).

kōwaha yawn.

kowata transparent.

kōwhā flash.

kōwhai flowering tree, *Sophora microphylla* and *S. tetraptera*; yellow.

kōwhai ngutu-kākā red kōwhai, parrot's bill, or kākā's beak, *Clianthus puniceus*.

kōwhaki tear off.

kōwhakiwhai flash frequently.

kōwhatu stone.

kowheka garment.

kowhera flash; open; yawn, gape.

kowheta writhe.

kōwhiri pick, choose, select.

kōwhiuwhiu fan.

kua word which indicates that action has been completed.

kūaha door; entrance.

kūaka common diving petrel, *Pelecanoides urinatrix*; eastern bar-tailed godwit, *Limosa lapponica*.

kūao young of animals.

kūare ignorant, stupid; worthless.

kuau beard.

kūhā thigh.

kuha gasp; ragged.

kuhu(-a,-ngia) enter; insert; put on clothes.

kuhukuhu pig.

kui polite form of address to female elder; grandma.

kuia female elder; old woman.

kūihi to speak softly.

kuihi goose.

kuihipere gooseberry.

kuini queen.

kuki cook.

kūkū New Zealand pigeon, *Hemiphaga novaeseelandiae*.

kuku(-a, kūngia) mussel, *Mytilus edulis, M. canaliculus,* etc; draw together; nip; nightmare.

kukume pull; persuade.

kukune grow; plump.

kūmara sweet potato, *Ipomomea batatas.*

kūmarahou shrub, *Pomaderris kumaraho.*

kume(-a) drag, pull; draw out.

kume-ā-papa gravity.

kūmera sweet potato, *Ipomomea batatas.*

kumete wooden bowl or trough.

kumikumi beard.

kūmore headland.

kumu buttocks.

kumukumu red gurnard, *Chelidonichthys kumu.*

kūpae sprat, *Sprattus antipodum, S. muelleri.*

kūpangopango dark in colour.

kūpapa lie flat, stoop; be neutral; side with the government, traitor (applied to Māori who fought alongside the government in the wars of the nineteenth century).

kūparu john dory, *Zeus faber.*

kupenga net.

kupu word; message; words spoken.

kupu matua headline.

kura chief; noted man of valour; glowing; red; red feathers; red ochre; precious; treasure; school.

kura kaupapa Māori state-funded total immersion Māori language school.

kura kōhungahunga kindergarten.

kura rata medical school.

kura tuarua secondary school.

kūpehe fold; wrinkle.

kūrae headland.

kūraruraru perplexed.

kurehe fold; wrinkle.

kurī dog.

kurī ārahi guide dog.

kurī tautiaki guard dog.

kurikuri spear-grass or wild spaniard, *Aciphylla* species.

kuru greenstone ornament; rap, thump; weary.

kurumatarērehu tattooed man.

kurupae beam.

kuruwhengi Australasian shoveler, *Anas rhynchotis.*

kuta rush or reed.

kūtai mussel, *Perna canaliculus.*

kūtere to rush to a place.

kuti (passive **kūtia**) draw together; nip; shut hand or mouth; nightmare.

kutikuti opening and shutting alternately; scissors; cut with scissors.

kutu louse; head-lice, nits; vermin.

kutukutu maggot; vermin.

kutukutu ahi nonsense.

kūwaha door; entrance.

kūware ignorant; worthless.

kūwhā thigh; connection by marriage.

kūwhewhewhewhe wrinkled.

M

mā and others (used for people, this word follows a noun or pronoun and has the effect of including others beyond those mentioned; frequently it has the effect of a plural); and (used to connect numerals to larger numbers); by way of; clean; for; go; pale; white; clear; introduces a conditional sentence (if).

mā te wā sometime, whenever.

Māehe March.

māeke cold.

māeneene smooth; soft.

maero fabulous monster; mile.

maha many; satisfied.

māhaki calm; loose; meek; quiet; mild.

mahaki invalid; ill, sick.

mahamaha liver.

mahana warm; temperature.

māhanga snare, trap; twins.

mahara be anxious; memory; remember; think about; thought.

māharahara think frequently of; anxious; worry; suppose.

māhau for you (singular).

mahau porch, verandah.

māhē sinker.

maheni magazine.

mahi(-a) act; business; deed; job; make; office; work.

mahi ā whare housework.

mahi kāinga homework.

mahi tahi co-operate.

mahihore peeled.

māhina moon.

mahinga kai cultivation, food source.

māhita teacher (master).

māhoe tree, whiteywood, *Melicytus ramiflorus*.

māhū gentle.

mahu healed.

mahue gone by; left behind; deserted; lost; passed on.

māhukihuki ceremonies to remove tapu from kūmara ground.

māhunga hair; head.

Mahuru September.

mai a word indicating some action being taken in the direction of or towards the speaker; from.

mai rā anō for ages, forever.

māia bold; brave; daring.

maiaka thin.

maianga rise up.

maiaorere fine cloak.

maihamo back of head.

maihao finger; toe.

maihi bargeboards of meeting house.

maiki depart; quietly.

maikuku claw; fingernail, toenail.

maimai aroha token of affection; song of mourning for dead.

maioha greet affectionately; welcome; gift.

maioro earthworks or fortifications of pā.

māipi wooden weapon.

maire tree, *Nestegis* species.

maire hau aromatic shrub, *Phebalium nudum.*

maire-tawake tree, *Syzygium maire.*

maitai iron (metal); dishes.

māitiiti young man.

mākā wild; shy.

maka(-ia) mug, cup; pass, throw.

makamaka small tree, *Ackama rosaefolia*; to throw about.

makara come; go; head.

makariri cold; frost; winter.

makau favourite; husband; wife.

makawe hair (of the head only).

mākekehu fair-headed.

mākere head.

makere fall; drop; alight; be lost.

mākeremumu winter.

maki invalid.

makimaki monkey.

makinui gorilla.

mako shark, *Isurus oxyrinchus*; shark tooth (worn as an ear-ornament).

makomako wineberry, *Aristotelia serrata*; bellbird, *Anthornis melanura.*

mākona having the appetite satisfied, full; replete.

mākū wet.

māku for me; I will.

mākūkū moist; damp.

makuku idle; pleasant tasting.

mākurakura pink.

mākutu bewitch; magic; spell; curse.

mākūware careless.

māmā light; quick; easy; simple; mum, mother.

mamae distress; pain; hurt.

mamaha steam.

mamaku black tree-fern *Cyathea medullaris.*

mamao distant.

mamaoa steam.

māminga deceive; deceitful; impose upon; make fun of; pretend.

māna for him; for her; he will, she will.

mana authority; influence; power; prestige.

mana motuhake self-government; personal freedom.

manaaki(-tia) look after, entertain; show respect or kindness; hospitality; hospitable.

manaakitanga hospitality.

manaia abstract carved figure.

manatunga keepsake.

manako to like; to long for.

manaia carved beaked figure.

manatu homesick.

mānawa mangrove, *Avicennia marina* var. *resinifera.*

manawa belly, stomach; bowels; breath; heart.

manawa hē heart attack.

manawanui brave; patient.

manawapā grudging; reluctant.

manawareka satisfied.

mānehenehe irritable.

Mane Monday.

manene stranger.

mānia plain (noun).

mania slippery; smooth; to slide.

maniheko nasty.

maninirau circus.

mano thousand; large number.

mānu float; overflow; be launched; be flooded.

manu bird; kite; start.
manu aute kite.
manu tukutuku kite.
manuhiri guest; visitor.
mānuka tea tree,
  Leptospermum scoparium.
mānukanuka worry; doubt;
  anxiety; anxious.
manukura chief; leader.
manumanu collar-bone.
manga branch; creek, stream;
  tributary; barracouta,
  Thyrsites atun; food scraps;
  green vegetables.
māngai mouth; agent;
  representative; spokesperson.
māngainga descendant.
mangeao tree, *Litsea calicaris.*
mangeo itch.
māngere lazy.
māngiongio chilblain.
mangō shark (various species).
mangu black.
mangungu crushed; uncooked.
mao we, us (myself and one
  other); to stop raining.
maoa cooked; ripe.
maonga cooked; ripe.
Māori the indigenous people of
  Aotearoa New Zealand;
  native, indigenous to
  Aotearoa New Zealand.
māori clear; fresh; ordinary.
māoritanga Māori culture;
  explanation; meaning.
māpau tree, *Myrsine australis.*
māpere marble.
mapi map.
māpou tree, *Myrsine australis.*
mapu flow freely; sigh; sob.
māra cultivated ground; farm;
  garden.
māra wāina vineyard.

mara form of address.
marae traditional Māori
  gathering place.
marae ātea open space in front
  of meeting house.
marakihau sea monster.
mārama natural light;
  understood; clear;
  transparent.
marama month; moon.
maramara splinter; chip.
maramara rīwai potato chips.
maramataka calendar.
maranga to arise; to get up.
marangai storm; heavy rain;
  east; east wind.
marara scattered; separated;
  umbrella.
mararī butterfish, *Odax pullus.*
mārau fork; pronged stick.
marau subject (school).
mārehe painstaking.
māreikura celestial female
  beings; woman of noble rank.
maremare cough.
mārena(-tia) marry.
mārenatanga marriage.
marere to drop.
mārie good omen; peaceful.
mārika carefully, quietly;
  certainly, quite.
marino calm.
maringi spill, be spilt; flow.
māripi knife.
mārire quiet; thoroughly;
  peaceful.
mārō hard; stiff; single-minded.
maro girdle; kilt-like garment;
  apron.
maroke dry.
māroki calm.
māroro destroyed; strong; flying
  fish, *Cypselurus lineatus.*

mārū gentle, calm.
marū bruised; crushed.
maru shade, shelter; sheltered; protection; power, authority.
mārua hollow; pit; valley; vacuum.
marumaru shaded.
mātā swamp.
matā flint, quartz; blade; lead; bullet; earwig.
mata face; surface; eye; edge; fresh; headland; raw; charm, spell; screen (computer).
mata kohore bleary-eyed.
mata renga bleary-eyed.
mataaho waka windscreen.
mataara keep awake, watchful; keep alert, keep watch; watchman.
mataati first.
mātai watch; inspect; gaze at; the sea.
matai black pine, *Prumnopitys taxifolia*.
mataika first person killed in battle.
mātaitai fish or food from sea or lake; salty.
matakahi wedge.
matakana wary.
matakerepō blind.
mātaki(-hia) look at, watch.
mātakitaki watch.
matakite divination; second sight; seer; prophecy.
matakoma swollen.
mataku afraid; fearful.
matakupenga fat covering the intestines.
matamata extremity; headland; summit.
matamatahuanga distant relative.

mātāmua eldest; first; main.
mātangatanga loose.
matangerengere cramped; numb.
matangi wind, breeze.
mātāngohi first person to be captured and killed in battle.
matangurunguru numb.
mātao cold.
mātaotao cool; to die out or become extinguished.
matapaia pottery.
matapihi window.
matapō blind.
mātāpono principle.
matapōrehu sadness.
mātāpuputu old people.
matara distant.
mātārae person of importance.
matarau many-pointed; fish spear.
matarekereke numb.
mātātā fern bird, *Bowdleria punctata*.
matatā carry on a litter.
matata open.
matatae clear up (of weather).
mātātahi young people.
matatau competent; expert.
matatira in a row.
mātau know; understand; knowledge; we, us (three or more people, excluding the people addressed).
matau hook; right-hand, right.
mātauranga knowledge; education.
matawai filled with tears, upset.
matawaia filled with tears, upset.
mātāwaka all tribes; all peoples.
matawhaia meet or strike by chance.

matawhāiti cautious.

mate danger; dead; death; due; ill; sickness, disease; sore; in love; suffering; in want of; to need; problem.

mate ā moa extinct.

mate huka diabetes.

mate koroputaputa smallpox.

mate manawa heart attack; heart disease.

mate pukupuku cancer.

mate wahine menstruation, period.

matekai hunger; hungry.

mātenga head.

matenga time or circumstance of death.

mātengatenga causing pain.

mateoha fond.

matewai thirst; thirsty.

māti match.

mātia spear.

matihao finger; toe.

matihe sneeze.

matikara finger; toe; measurement of length (finger-span).

matikuku claw; fingernail; toenail; hoof.

matimati toe; finger.

matipou tree, *Myrsine australis*.

matira fishing rod.

mātirakahu Chatham Island rail, *Gallirallus modestus* (extinct).

mātiti split; summer.

mātoro woo.

mātoru crowd.

mātotoru thick.

mātotoru o te waka (heavy) traffic.

mātou we, us (three or more people, excluding the people addressed).

matū fat.

mātua first; important; main body of an army; must.

matua (plural **mātua**) adult; division of an army; father; important; main; parent.

matua kēkē aunt; uncle.

matua tāne father; uncle.

matua wahine mother; aunt.

matua whāngai foster parent.

mātuhi bush wren, *Xenicus longipes* (extinct).

matuku-hūrepō Australasian bittern, *Botaurus poiciloptilus*.

matuku-moana white-faced heron, *Ardea novaehollandiae*; reef heron, *Egretta sacra*.

mātūtū convalescent.

māu for you (singular); you will.

mau(-ria) bring, carry; bear.

mau caught; fixed; lasting; take up; take hold of, seize; use.

mau herehere hostage; prisoner.

mau kakī necklace.

mau taringa ear pendants.

māua we, us (the speaker and one other).

mauāhara hate; hatred.

mauī left; left-hand.

māuiui sick; tired, exhausted.

maumahara remember.

maumau to no purpose; waste.

māunu bait.

maunu come out; be drawn.

maunutanga migration.

maunga mountain.

mauri life principle; principle; talisman.

mauri moe unconscious.

mautohe protest.
mawehe to be separated.
māwhe faded; subsided.
māwhero pink.
mawhiti to leap; to skip.
māwhitiwhiti grasshopper.
me and; if; with; like; should.
mea(-tia, meinga) do; fact;
    make; one; reason; say; thing;
    think; which; who; wish;
    someone; persons.
mea ake soon.
mea kau ake immediately; very
    soon.
meāke (mea ake) soon.
meamea bastard; order.
mehemea if.
Mei May.
mei if; judging by.
mekari close to.
meke to punch; fist.
mekepaoro volleyball.
mema member.
mema pāremata member of
    parliament (MP).
memeha dissolved; listless,
    weak.
menā if.
mene assemble.
menemene to smile; to make a
    face.
meneti minute.
menge withered.
mēra mail.
mere short flat weapon made of
    stone or greenstone.
merekara miracle.
merengi melon.
mētara metal.
mīere honey.
mīharo(-tia) admire; be
    surprised; wonder at;
    wonderful.

mihi greet; greeting; lament;
    praise; acknowledge, thank;
    miss.
mihimihi greetings and
    introductions.
mihinare missionary; Anglican.
mīhini machine, machinery;
    motor.
mīhini hoko vending machine.
mīhini keri digger.
mihingare missionary;
    Anglican.
mimi urine; to urinate.
mimiti dried up; swallowed up.
minamina desire, wish for.
mine be gathered together.
minita minister.
mingimingi shrub, *Cyathodes
    juniperina*; shrub, *Coprosma
    propinqua*; shrub,
    Leucopogon fasciculata.
mingo wrinkled.
mingomingo kata smile.
miraka milk.
miri rub, wipe; stroke; soothe.
mirihau windsurfing.
mirimiri massage.
mirimita millimetre.
miririta millilitre.
miro tree, *Prumnopitys
    ferruginea*; spin; thread; twist;
    whirlpool.
miromiro North Island tomtit,
    Petroica macrocephala.
mirumiru bubbles.
mita mister; metre.
mītara measles.
mīti meat.
mīti hipi mutton.
mīti kau beef.
mitimiti to lick.
mō concerning; for; for the use
    of; in consideration of;

indicates future time; in preparation of; instead of.

moa flightless bird (various species, extinct); garden bed.

moana sea; ocean; lake.

moari swing, or giant stride, frequently erected on the bank of a river or pool.

moata early; early morning.

moe marry; sleep; nap.

moehewa dream.

moemoeā dream.

moenga bed, mattress; marriage.

moenga tara marriage terminated by death.

moeone grub.

moepapa nightmare.

moeriki Dieffenbach's rail, *Gallirallus dieffenbachi* (extinct).

moetāhae adultery.

mohimohi pilchard, *Sardinops neopilchardus.*

mōhio(-tia) know, recognise; to be suspicious; understand; intelligent, clever; wise.

mōhiotanga knowledge.

moho stupid.

mohoa to the present time.

moho-pererū banded rail, *Gallirallus philippensis.*

mōhū selfish.

mōhua yellowhead, *Mohoua ochrocephala.*

moi call to summon dog.

mōkai pet; prisoner; slave; youngest.

mokamokai tame animal or bird; dried human head.

moke solitary; solitary person; hermit; monk.

mokemoke lonely.

moki blue moki, *Latridopsis ciliaris.*

mōkī bundle; package; raft made of flax stalks or rushes.

mōkihi bundle; package; raft made of flax stalks or rushes.

moko lizard; monster, person (figurative); reptile; traditional tattooing.

moko ngārara crocodile.

mokomoko head; lizard.

mokopuna grandchild (including great-niece and great-nephew); descendant; children.

mokotuauri dinosaur.

mokoweri dinosaur.

mōku for me.

momi suck.

momo type; breed; descendant.

momoe keeping the eyes shut.

mōmona fat (as opposed to thin); fertile; rich (food).

momori bare; smooth.

momote greedily; in secret; severely.

mōna for him; for her.

monamona knuckle; joint.

moni money, cash; coin.

moni whiwhi income.

mongamonga crushed.

more bare; plain, not decorated; toothless.

mōrearea dangerous.

mōrehu survivor.

moremore bald.

mōrere swing or giant stride.

mōri person of low birth.

morihana goldfish.

moroki continuing.

moroki noa nei up to the present time.

mōrunga lifted up.

mōteatea traditional song; lament; mourning; fearful; hesitation.

mōtēra motel.

moto(-kia) strike with fist; blow.

motokā motor car.

motopaika motor cycle.

motū steak.

motu(-hia) cut; island; nation; national; severed; grove of trees.

motuhake independent; separate; separated; special; different.

motuhuka iceberg.

motukā motor car.

motunga quota.

motupaika motorbike.

moturere broken or cut off.

mōu for you.

mōua back of neck.

moumou to no purpose; waste.

moumouranga betrothal; connection by marriage; marriage.

moutere island.

mōwhiti glasses, spectacles; hoop; ring.

mōwhiti rā sunglasses.

mū insect.

mua before; first; front; the past.

muanga eldest child.

muheni insult.

mui to swarm.

muka flax fibre.

mukākā(-tia) annoy, irritate.

muku wipe, rub; rubber, eraser.

mūmū silence; taciturn person.

mumu valiant warrior.

muna darling; relate confidentially; secret, mystery; hide.

mura flame; blaze.

muramura flash; bright-coloured.

muri after; afterwards; north; rear; the future.

muri tata iho shortly afterwards.

murikōkai back of the head.

muringa afterwards; youngest child.

muritai sea breeze.

muriwai backwater; lagoon.

muru(-a) forgive; gather; plunder; rub; wipe.

mutu ended; finished.

mutunga concluding; conclusion; end; finish.

mutunga ika last person killed in battle.

mutunga wiki weekend.

mutunga rawa maximum.

mutumutu mutilate.

N

nā belonging to; by; by way of, through; an adverb indicating nearness to the person addressed, near you; used at beginning of sentence to attract attention, and then.

nā konā because of that.

nā konei because of this.

nā reira therefore.

naenae mosquito.

naeroa mosquito.

nahea what time (used of the past).

Nāhinara National (political party).

nāianei now, soon, today.

naihi knife.

naka indicates position near the person spoken to, near you.

nākahi snake.

nāku I (past tense); mine.

nama number; owe; bill, invoice.

namata olden times.

namu sandfly, *Austrosimulium* species.

nānā care for, look after.

nāna his, her (singular); he, she (past tense); who.

nanā! look!

nana eyebrow.

nanahi yesterday.

nanakia reckless; crafty; fierce; naughty; treacherous.

nanekoti goat.

nanenane goat.

nani wild cabbage; wild turnip.

nao feel; to handle.

nape jerk; speak falteringly; weave.

napō last night.

napuka shrub, *Hebe speciosa.*

nati pinch; nut.

natinati pinched; stifled.

natu scratch (noun).

nāu yours (singular); you (past tense).

nau mai welcome.

nauhea fellow; rascal.

nāwai soon; eventually; for some time.

nawe scar.

nē expression giving emphasis to a question: isn't it?, really?

neha sleep lightly, doze.

nehenehe forest.

neherā olden times.

nehu(-a) bury (of a corpse).

nei adverb indicating nearness to speaker.

neinei shrub, *Dracophyllum latifolium.*

neke move.

nekeneke move gradually; move along.

nenewha shut the eyes.

nēra nail.

neti toy dart.

niao edge; rim; top plank of canoe.

niho tooth.

niho tunga toothache.

nīkau palm, *Rhopalostylis sapida.*

niti toy dart.

niu divination; small sticks used

in divining; pole set up for Hauhau ceremonies.

Niu Tīreni New Zealand.

niwha bravery; bold; rage; barb.

nō belonging to; from; from the time that; in; on account of, because of; when.

nō hea? from where?

nō konā because of that, therefore.

nō konei because of this, therefore.

nō reira therefore.

nō tahirā the day before yesterday.

nō te mea because.

nō whea? from where?

noa free from tapu (denotes the absence of limitations of various kinds); used to intensify some adverbs; already; at all; completely; just; merely, ordinary.

noa iho just, only; completely.

Noema November.

nohinohi small.

noho(-ia) live; sit; stay; inhabit.

noho puni camp.

nohoanga seat; temporary camp; home.

nohopuku diet; be silent.

noi elevated; high; on high.

noke worm.

noko stern of canoe.

nōku I (past tense); mine.

nōnahea? when? (used of the past).

nōnāianei now; today.

nōnakuanei a little while ago.

nōnamata a long time ago.

nōnanahi yesterday.

nonaoake the day before yesterday.

nōnaoakenui three days ago.

nōnapō last night.

nōnatahirā the day before yesterday.

nōnawhea? when? (used of the past).

nonohi small (plural).

nonoke judo.

noti contract; pinch.

nōu yours; you (past tense).

nui abundant; great; big, large; many; important; publicly; quantity; size; widely.

nui te utu expensive.

nuinga majority; most; gathering.

nuka deceive; strategem.

nukarau deceive.

nuke crooked.

nuku distance; move, shift; move along; extend.

nukunuku remove.

nunui large (plural).

nunumi disappear.

nūpepa newspaper.

NG

ngā the (plural).
ngā tini a Tāne wildlife.
ngaengae heel.
ngaere to quake or shiver; soft, ripe; to roll.
ngaeroa mosquito.
ngāhae dawn.
ngahau amusing, enjoying, entertaining.
ngahengahe forest; weak.
ngahere bush; forest.
ngāherehere bush; forest.
ngahiri pounder for fern-root.
ngāhoahoa headache.
ngahoro to fall; more.
ngahu clear; distorted.
ngahuru autumn (harvest time); old word for 10.
ngāi prefix meaning tribe or clan, e.g. Ngāi Tahu.
ngaio tree, *Myoporum laetum*.
ngākau feelings; heart (figurative); vitals.
ngākaukore disinclined.
ngākaunui eager, keen.
ngākaurua uncertain, in two minds.
ngaki avenge; to plant; to weed; to cultivate.
ngakinga cultivated ground, garden.
ngako fat (as on meat).
ngana breathe heavily; intent; persist; rage; screech.
ngāngā breathe heavily; make a noise; screech.
nganga stone of fruit; hail; shell; husk.
ngangare quarrel; urge.

ngao a shoot.
ngaoko move slightly.
ngārā them; they.
ngārara monster; reptile; insect.
ngārara arikata alligator.
ngare blood relations; family; send; urge.
ngari annoyance.
ngaro absent; destroyed; disappeared; extinct; forgotten; hidden; invisible; lessened; lost; enter; blowfly, fly.
ngaru wave.
ngaruiti microwave.
ngāruru headache.
ngata slug; snail; speck; with difficulty; satisfied.
ngātahi together.
ngāti prefix denoting tribe or clan, e.g. Ngāti Porou.
ngau affect; bite; hurt; wander.
ngāueue shake.
ngaungau chew.
ngāwari soft, supple, flexible; softly; accommodating, kind, easy-going, tolerant; easy, simple; cheap.
ngāwhā boiling spring.
ngawhi punished.
ngāwhāriki boiling spring.
ngē noise; word used in several contexts without altering the sense.
ngehengehe soft; weak.
ngehingehi bag used for expressing oil from seeds.
ngenge tired; weariness.
ngenge rererangi jet lag.

ngeri derisive chant with actions.

ngeru cat.

ngia seem.

ngiha burn; fire.

ngira needle.

ngirungiru South Island tomtit, *Petroica macrocephala*.

ngoengoe scream.

ngohengohe soft; pliable; easy.

ngohi fish.

ngoi energy; strength.

ngoikore weak; weakness.

ngoio asthma; whistling noise.

ngōiro conger eel, *Conger verreauxi*.

ngōki creep, crawl.

ngongengonge crippled.

ngongo dimple; sick person; tube; waste away.

ngongohā snorkel.

ngongore blunt (without barb).

ngongoro exclaim with admiration or wonder; snore.

ngore flexible.

ngota atom; fragment; particle.

ngotangota smashed to powder.

ngoto head.

ngū silent, dumb, speechless; one who is unable to swim; squid.

ngungu turn aside.

ngunguru murmur; rumble; sigh; suppressed groan.

nguru nose-flute.

ngutu beak; lip; mouth of river.

ngutu hore wasteful.

ngutu huia talkative person.

ngutu momoho abusive; talkative.

ngutu pārera pistol.

ngutu tere false, untrustworthy.

ngutuawa mouth of river.

O

ō of; forming possessive (plural); from; the place of; your (plural).

ō kōrua your (plural, addressed to two people).

ō koutou your (plural, addressed to three or more people).

ō mātou our (plural, their and my).

ō māua our (plural, his or her and my).

ō rātou their (plural, three or more people).

ō rāua their (plural, two people).

ō tātou our (plural).

ō tāua our (plural, your and my).

oha dying speech; keepsake; greet; increase.

ōhākī dying speech.

ohaoha abundant; generosity; generous.

oho to jump; to start with surprise; to wake.

ohooho cherished; panic; requiring care.

ohorere start suddenly.

ohotata emergency.

ohu working bee of volunteers.

ohu-rapa search party.

ōi sooty shearwater or muttonbird, *Puffinus griseus*; grey-faced petrel, *Pterodroma macroptera*; soft mud; shout.

oi agitate; move continuously (as the sea); shudder.

oinga childhood; youth.

oioi shake gently.

oka dagger; prick; stab; yam.

okaoka stab.

oke invalid; wriggle.

okeoke toss about.

Oketopa October.

okioki to pause; to rest.

okooko to nurse.

ōku my (plural).

oma(-kia) escape; run.

oma taumano marathon.

omanga refuge.

ōna his, her (plural).

onamata of time past.

one beach; sand; mud.

oneone earth, soil.

onepū sand.

oneuku clay.

onewa stone weapon.

ono six.

ongaonga nettle, *Urtica ferox*.

ope travelling group; war party.

opeti crowded.

opua verandah (or porch) of a whare.

ora alive; escape; healthy; safe; satisfied; slave; survive; unhurt; wedge; well; life.

oraiti escaping with difficulty.

oranga life; livelihood; survivor; welfare.

ori hīteki ballet.

orihou shrub or small tree, *Pseudopanax colensoi*.

oriori lullaby.

ōrite equal; the same as, identical; similar.

oro sharpen; grind.

ōroko as soon as; but now; for the first time; just.

orotahi note (music).

ota uncooked; unripe.

otaota rubbish; vegetables; vegetation; weeds.

oti indicates that action is completed, finished; else.

otirā but; but at the same time.

ōu your (plural, addressed to one person).

ouou few.

P

pā(-kia,-ngia) fortification, stockade; village; block up; to blow; form of address to male elder or superior; be heard; hit; strike; be struck; obstruct; touch; affect.

pā hirahira castle.

pā tuna eel weir.

pae lie across, rest; gums; horizon; horizontal ridge; region; shelf; pie.

pae patopato typewriter.

pae tere speed limit.

paekura lost property.

paemanu collar-bone.

paenga shipwreck.

Paengawhāwhā April.

paepae bar; beam; bench at the front of a meeting house, front row of seats.

paeroa range of hills; wind which blows along the shore.

Paeroa-o-Whānui the Milky Way.

paewai collarbone; jawbone; person of importance; species of eel.

pāhake adult; old man.

pahaki fail; slip.

pāhau beard.

paheke fail; slip; slide.

pāhekeheke slippery; uncertain.

pahemo pass by; pass on.

pāhi boss; purse, wallet; bag, handbag, pack; suitcase; pass; past.

pahī adventure; party of travellers; person of low birth; slave.

pahi bus.

pahi iti minibus.

pāhihi passenger.

pāhiketepōro basketball.

pāho broadcast, get around; soaring.

pāhoahoa back of the head; headache.

pahū bomb; burglar alarm; burst; explode; wooden gong.

pahū ahi fireworks.

pāhunu anxiety; burn; fire.

pahure escape; pass by; be carried out successfully.

pai(-ngia) good, okay; to like; pleasant; satisfactory; suitable; be willing.

pai ake better.

pai atu better.

paiaka root of tree; weapon made from root of tree.

paiheneti percent.

paihere bundle.

paihikara bicycle.

paihikara maunga mountain bike.

pāike strike.

pāina to dry; warm oneself; sunbathe.

paina pine tree.

painga benefit.

paipa pipe; cigarette.

Paipera Tapu Holy Bible.

paitini poison.

pāka box; park.

paka quarrel.

pakahā fluttering shearwater, *Puffinus gavia*.

pakakau xylophone.

pakakina glowing.
pakanga battle; war; fight.
Pakanga Tuarua Second World War.
Pakanga Tuatahi First World War.
pakapaka baked hard; heatwave.
pakaru break; broken; shattered; split.
pākatio freezer.
pākau kite; wing.
pākaurua short-tailed stingray, *Dasyatis brevicaudatus*.
pake obstinate.
Pākehā foreign; foreigner (usually applied to white person); English; New Zealand European; Western.
pākeho limestone.
pākehokeho slippery.
pakeke hard, stiff; difficult; adult, elder.
pakepakeha awkward; disorderly.
paketai driftwood; anything cast up by the sea.
pākete bucket.
pākī hamburger.
paki clap; fine, sunny; slap; buggy.
pakiaka root.
pākihi desert; barren land.
pakihi business.
pakihiwi shoulder; measurement, the distance from the fingertips of one hand along the arm to the other shoulder.
pakikau fin; garment; wing.
pākiki to question often.
pakipaki clap, applause; famous; stories.

pākira bald.
pakitara gossip; wall of a house.
pakituri hitch-hiker.
pākiwaha boasting.
pakiwaitara legend; scandal; tale.
pakiwaituhi cartoon.
pakiwara naked; scantily clothed.
pakō blistered; make a loud sound.
pākoko barren; childless.
pākoko tawhito brave; warrior.
pakū make sharp or sudden sound; resound.
paku dried; small.
pakupaku small.
pākuru chant song to the accompaniment of sticks knocked together; knock.
pāmamao distant.
pāmārō solid; steady.
pāmu farm.
pana(-ina,-ia, panā) drive away; expel; press, push; a switch.
panana banana.
panatahi odd number.
pane head.
pane kuini postage stamp.
paneke to advance; goal (sport); to score.
panekeke pancake.
panekoti petticoat; skirt.
pani to block up; bereaved person; orphan; to paint; to smear, to spread.
pani ngutu lipstick.
paniaku toothpaste.
panikakā mustard.
pānui(-tia) advertise; advertisement; message;

newsletter; notice; read aloud; read.

pānuitanga announcement.

panuku next; sledge.

pānga tuhituhi stationery.

panga(-ina, pangā) lay; throw; place; pass; puzzle; riddle.

pānganga thin.

pāngarau mathematics.

pangare beardless.

pango black.

pao(-a) break; sing; a type of song; strike, pound.

paoa smoke (from a fire).

paoka pierce; stab; fork.

paoro echo; ball; pool.

pāpā dad, father.

papā burst, explode.

papa board; buttocks; earth; flat rock; floor; ground; plane (mathematics); shell; anything hard and flat.

papa angaanga skull.

papa kararehe zoo.

papa pānui noticeboard.

papa tuhituhi blackboard, whiteboard.

papa-ahu skull.

pāpāho broadcast; media.

pāpāho maha multimedia.

papai good (plural).

pāpaka crab.

papakāinga ancestral settlement.

papaki smack.

pāpaku shallow.

papakupu dictionary.

papanga layer.

pāpango dark in colour; New Zealand scaup or black teal, *Aythya novaeseelandiae*.

pāpapa husk; shell.

pāpapa kōpure ladybird.

papapātua baskets or vessels of totara bark.

pāpara father (this word denotes a true father).

pāparakāuta hotel, pub.

papareti skateboard.

paparewa thin; in poor condition.

pāpāringa cheek.

papāroa scarce.

papatākaro playing field; playground.

papatāniwhaniwha plant, *Lagenophora pumila*.

pāpātanga rate, speed.

papataunga runway.

papatipu native land without European title.

papatū bulwark.

papatupu native land without European title.

papī blind.

pāpuni dam; dried up.

pāpura purple.

parā rotten.

para blood relation; frostfish, *Lepidopus caudatus*; pollen; sediment.

para whakawai training with weapons.

pārae open country; field, paddock; park.

paraehe brush.

parahanga litter, rubbish.

pāraharaha flat.

paraheahea helpless; lazy; ugly.

parāhi brass.

parai fry; frying pan.

paraihe award, prize; brush.

paraihe niho toothbrush.

paraikete blanket.

Paraire Friday.

paraire bridle.
parakau slave.
parakimete blacksmith.
parakipere blackberry.
parakuihi breakfast.
paramanawa refreshments; snack.
paramu plum.
parani daisy.
parangia to be overtaken by sleep.
parāoa sperm whale, *Physeter macrocephalus*; bread; flour.
parāoa parai fried bread.
parāoa rimurapa pasta.
parāoa roa weapon made of whale rib.
paraone brown.
parapara bird-catching shrub or small tree, *Pisonia brunonianum*; filth; talents.
pararā broad-billed prion, *Pachyptila vittata*.
pararau slave.
pararē to speak loudly.
parareka potato.
parataniwha herb, *Elatostema rugosum*.
paratū high up.
parau false; falsehood, lie; plough.
parawaha spittle.
pāre barley.
pare bodice; head ornament; top-knot; carved lintel of doorway.
pare tīkākā sunscreen.
parehe pizza.
pareho skull.
pārekareka enjoyable; pleasant; spotted shag, *Phalacrocorax punctatus*.

parekura battle; battlefield; people killed in battle; disaster.
pāremata parliament.
paremo drowned.
parenga riverbank.
pārera grey duck, *Anas superciliosa*.
parerori cramp.
paretai riverbank.
pari cliff; high or flowing tide.
pārihirihi skull.
parirau wing.
paritū steep.
pārō hollow of hand; skull.
pārongo hearing aid.
parori sprained; crooked.
pāroro cloudy; storm.
paru dirt; dirty; messy, untidy; excrement; mud.
pārunga upstairs.
paruparu shellfish ready for cooking; mud, dirt; dirty, discoloured; mess.
pata drop of water; butter.
pata kai cereal.
patahinu margarine.
patahua muesli.
pātai(-a) ask; enquire; question.
pātaka elevated storehouse; pantry.
pātangatanga starfish.
patapata drip, drop.
patapatai to question, interrogate.
pātara bottle.
pātari amuse; entice; provoke.
pāteke brown teal, *Anas chlorotis*.
pātene button.
pātere song of derision.
patere flow freely; many.

patete five finger, *Schefflera digitata*.
pātiki sand flounder, *Rhombosolea plebeia*; paddock.
pātiki rori common sole, *Peltorhamphus novaezelandiae*.
patiko hastily.
patipati flatter, sweet-talk; flattery.
pātītī grass.
pātōtara shrub, *Cyathodes juniperina*.
pātōtō beat; knock.
pātotoi cracked.
patu(-a) beat; hit; kill; wall; weapon; racquet, bat (for sports).
patu parāoa short flat weapon made from bone of whale.
patupaiarehe fairy.
pau consumed; exhausted; complete, exhaustive.
pāua mollusc (inside surface of shell is iridescent), *Haliotis* species.
paukena pumpkin.
pauku thick cape which acted as armour against spear thrusts.
pāuna pound.
paunga rāwhitu weekend.
paura powder.
pāwera afraid; solicitous.
pāwerawera awe; dread.
pāwhara tear open; smoked (of fish).
pāwhero red-haired.
pea perhaps, maybe; probably; bear; pear.
pea hurumā polar bear.
peara pearl.

peha boast; skin.
pēhanga heap.
pēhea? how?; act in what way?; of what kind?
pēhi(-a) press; oppress; repress.
pehi waylay.
pei(-a) drive out.
peihana basin.
peita paint.
peka branch; cheek.
pēkana bacon.
pekapeka long-tailed bat, *Chalinolobus tuberculatus*; short-tailed bat, *Mystacina tuberculata*; greenstone ornament.
pēke bag; bank; sack; pocket; sachet.
peke completed; jump; limb; shoulder.
pekerangi ozone layer.
peki chirping.
pēnā so; in that way; like that.
pene pen; penny.
pene pura ballpoint pen.
pene rākau pencil.
pēnei like this.
penupenu mashed.
pepa paper; pepper; print-out.
pepa whēru toilet paper.
pēpē soft mass.
pēpe baby.
pepe flutter; butterfly.
pepeha aphorism; proverb; quotation; witticism.
pepeke frog.
pēpepe butterfly; moth.
pēpi baby.
Pēpuere February.
pērā same as that, like that.
pere arrow; dart; throw dart by means of stick and string; bell.

pere rua yacht.
perehi press; print.
perehina bristle.
pereki brick.
pereti plate.
peruperu eyebrows.
petapeta all together.
peti heap up.
pewa bow-shaped; eyebrow; raise the eyebrows.
pēwhea how?; act in what way?; of what kind?
pī eye; bee; pea.
pī rorohū bumblebee.
pia gel; gum; sap; beer; undergraduate student; apprentice.
pia kano crayon.
piako empty; hollow.
piana piano.
piari hunchback; anyone deformed.
pīata bright; clear; shine; shiny.
piau axe; iron.
pīauau knife.
piha gills.
pīhanga window.
piharau lamprey, *Geotria australis.*
pihareinga cricket (insect).
piharoa hatchet; iron.
pihepihe girdle.
pīhi piece.
pihi shoot, sprout; waterproof.
pihikete biscuit.
pīhoihoi New Zealand pipit, *Anthus novaeseelandiae.*
pīhopa bishop.
pika a pick.
pīkaokao chicken.
pīkau carry on back; load for back; take responsibility for.
pīkaunga mountaineering.

pīkete biscuit.
piki assist; climb; climb over; helper; press close together; tightly curled hair.
piki toka rock-climbing.
pikiarero bush clematis, *Clematis paniculata.*
pikiniki picnic.
pikitanga ascent of hill.
pikitia picture; movie, film; pictures, cinema.
piko bend; bent; corner; curve; curved.
pīkoko hungry.
pikopiko winding about.
pīhaki implement for weeding.
pīnakitanga gentle slope.
pīnati peanut
pīnati pata peanut pata.
pine close together; pin.
pine pin.
pinepine little.
pīnohi tongs.
pīnono beg.
pīngao seaside plant used in weaving, *Desmoschoenus spiralis.*
pīoi see-saw.
piopio New Zealand thrush, *Turnagra capensis* (extinct).
pīpī chick; baby.
pipi mollusc, *Amphidesma australis.*
pipiha snore.
pīpipi brown creeper, *Mohoua novaeseelandiae.*
Pipiri June (the first month of the Māori year).
pipiri cling together; winter.
pīpīwharauroa shining cuckoo, *Chrysococcyx lucidus.*
pīrangi(-tia) desire; to desire; want.

pirau decay; extinguished; pus; rotten.
pire bill; pill.
piri cling; keep close; to hide; waterproof, watertight.
pirihi priest.
pirihimana police; police officer.
pirikoko mystery.
pirimia prime minister.
piriniha prince; princess.
piripiri biddy-biddy, *Acaena* species; velcro.
piripoho baby.
pirita mistletoe, *Tupeia antarctica*; supplejack, *Ripogonum scandens*.
piriti bridge; priest.
piro bad smell; intestines; stinking.
pītakataka gymnastics.
pītiti peach.
pito at first; end; navel, belly-button.
pitoiti almost.
pītoitoi robin, *Petroica australis*.
pito-toto blood relation.
piu skipping; throw; step; jump.
piupiu skirt-like garment; common hard fern, *Blechnum* species.
pīwa fever.
pīwaiwaka North Island fantail, *Rhipidura fuliginosa placabilis*; South Island fantail, *R.f. fuliginosa*.
pīwakawaka North Island fantail, *Rhipidura fuliginosa placabilis*; South Island fantail, *R.f. fuliginosa*.
piwari beautiful; pliant.
pō night; chaos; darkness; place of the dead.

pō mārie good night.
pō whakangahau concert, party.
poa bait; food; mouth and throat.
poaka pig; pork; pied stilt, *Himantopus himantopus*.
poaka kini guinea pig.
pōānini giddy.
pōangaanga skull.
poari board.
poataniwha shrub, *Melicope simplex*.
pōhā youngest child; food container made from kelp; pastry.
pōhara poor.
pōhatu stone, pebble.
pōhauhau confused.
pohe blind.
pōhēhē mistaken; perplexed; unsuspecting.
pohepohe distracted, inattentive.
pohewa imagine.
pōhiri(-tia) beckon; to wave; welcome.
poho abdomen; bosom; chest.
pōhue bindweed, *Calystegia sepium*.
pōhutukawa Christmas tree, *Metrosideros excelsa*.
poi ball; light ball attached to flax string; lock of hair.
poihau balloon.
poikiri soccer.
poikōpiko table tennis.
poka hole; force one's way; trespass; to cut out, to tear out; to gut.
poka noa to act in a random manner.
poka tata short-cut.

pōkai flock; roll up, wind up, wrap around; swarm; travel around.

pōkaikaha confused; in doubt.

pōkaitara band of warriors.

pōkākā tree, *Elaeocarpus dentatus*.

pokake presumptuous.

pokanga operation (surgical).

pokapū agency; centre.

pōkarekare to be agitated (of liquid).

pōkē dark; dirty; gloomy.

poke(-a) dirty; mix; pollute.

poke parāoa to make bread.

pōkēao dark cloud.

pōkēkohu mix with water or fluid.

pokenga pollution.

pokere in the dark.

pokerehū unintentionally.

pokerenoa recklessly.

pokihiwi shoulder.

pokohiwi shoulder.

pokorua ant; pit.

pokotaringa ear.

pokowhiwhi shoulder.

pōkuru throw.

pōma bomb.

pona cord; knot; tie in knot; ankle; knuckle.

ponaturi mythical beings who sleep on land, but retire under the sea during the daytime.

poniponi pony; small.

pono true; faithful; truth; honest, reliable.

pononga chattels; prisoner; servant; slave; true.

pōnga nightfall.

ponga silver fern, *Cyathea dealbata*.

pongāihu nostril.

pongaponga nostril.

pongere stifling.

pōpō pat with the hand; soothe.

popō crowd.

popo decay; rotten.

pōpokotea whitehead, *Mohoua albicilla*.

popoki cover; cover over; knee-cap; lid; spread over.

poporo covet; mean.

pora large, sea-going canoe; foreigner; stranger.

poraka block; frog; jersey, jumper; sweatshirt.

poraka taratara toad.

pōrangi crazy, mad; idiot; seek.

pōrearea nuisance; interfere; disturb; modest.

pōrera floor mat.

pōria ring of bone on leg of bird; ornament; to load.

pōrihirihi skull.

pōriro illegitimate child, bastard.

pōro ball.

poro a slice; broken off; a piece broken off.

poroaki leave instructions on parting.

pōrohe messy, untidy.

porohita circle; ring; wheel.

porohuri overturn, upset.

porokaiwhiria pigeonwood, *Hedycarya arborea*.

porokakī neck, throat.

poropiti prophet.

poroporo shrub, *Solanum aviculare* ('bulli-bull'); bracelet; purple.

poroporoaki farewell speech; take leave of, say goodbye to; a tribute to someone who has died.

pororaru bewildered.

pōrorotua cramped; numb; weak.
pororua meddle with.
porotiti disc; rotate.
porowhawhe merry-go-round.
porowhita circle; ring; wheel.
pōrutu splash.
pōtae cap, hat; head covering; hood.
pōtae mārō helmet.
pōtaka spinning top.
pōtari snare.
pōtarotaro lawnmower.
pōti election; vote.
poti boat; cat.
poti paku dinghy.
pōtiki child; youngest child.
potipoti shrimp.
poto short.
potopoto short.
pōturi deaf; slow.
pou pole; post; support.
pou koki stilts.
pou niho dentist.
pou tātū main post of house.
pou tokomanawa middle post of house.
pou turu stilts.
pōua grandfather; male elder; old person.
pouaka a small container on a post for holding valuable possessions; box; suitcase.
pouaka poutāpeta post-office box.
pouaka reta letter box.
pouaka whakaata television.
pouaru widow; widower.
pounamu greenstone; greenstone weapon; bottle; dark green.
poupou father-in-law;
mother-in-law; old people; peg; post (especially carved post in meeting house); steep.
poupoutanga o te rā midday.
pourewa elevated platform.
pōuri dark; sad, unhappy; sorry.
pōuriuri gloomy; very dark; brown.
poururu frown; gloomy.
pōuruuru sleepy.
poutāpeta post office.
pōuto cut off.
poutoko ture lawyer.
poutokomanawa centre post in meeting house.
poutoti stilts.
Poutūterangi March.
pouwhenua weapon resembling quarterstaff.
pōwhiri(-tia) beckon; to wave; welcome.
pū blow gently; bunch; cause, foundation, origin, root, source; double; exact, precise; flute; gun; heap; tribe; tube; very; wise person.
pua flower; seed.
pūaha mouth of river.
pūahi dogskin cloak.
puaki come out.
pūangi balloon.
pūao dawn.
pua-o-te-reinga plant, *Dactylanthus taylori*.
puare exposed; open; displayed; hole, opening.
puatawhiwhi rātā vine, *Metrosideros fulgens*.
puāwai flower; grey hair.
puawānanga clematis, *Clematis paniculata*.
puea avenged; to float up.
puehu dust.

pūhā green vegetable, sow-thistle, *Sonchus oleraceus*.

pūhaehae envy, jealousy.

pūhana glow.

puhi betrothed; bunch of feathers; much-admired young woman, virgin; post used in ceremonial magic; to tie in bunches; topknot.

puhipuhi blow or puff frequently; to smoke.

pūhoi slow; blunt.

pūhore omen of ill-success in hunting.

pūhuki blunt.

pūhungahunga rough, unfinished.

pūhuruhuru hairy.

puia hot spring; volcano.

puka broad-leafed tree, *Griselinia lucida*; cabbage; spade.

pūkaea large wooden wind instrument.

pūkaha engine.

pūkai to lie in a heap.

pūkana to stare with bulging eyes.

pūkanohi eye.

pukapuka book; letter; paper; rangiora shrub, *Brachyglottis repanda*: this shrub has white undersides to its leaves, hence book etc (the leaves of the rangiora were used for writing on when paper was scarce in the early days of Pākehā settlement); lungs.

pukapuka pakiwaituhi comic book.

pukatea tree, *Laurelia novaezelandiae*.

puke hill.

pūkei to lie in a heap.

pūkēkē arm; armpit.

pūkeko swamp hen; *Porphyrio melanotus*.

pūkenga expert, knowledgeable; professor; skill; skilled; well-versed.

pukepuke hilly; small hill.

pūkohu mist.

pūkōrero orator.

pūkoro pocket.

puku abdomen; boil; stomach; swelling; secretly; without speaking.

pukumahi hard-working.

pukupā barren; childless.

pukupuku closely woven mat, impervious to weapons when dampened.

pukuriri anger, fury, rage; furious.

pukutākaro full of fun; playful.

pūmanawa rorohiko software.

pūmau constant.

pūmuka stab.

puna hole; spring of water; wife; fountain.

punawētā Māori may, *Carpodetus serratus*.

pune spoon.

pūnehu mist; misty.

punenga kupu word processor.

puni camp; company; crowd; dam.

pūniho gums.

pūnu spoon.

punua young of animal.

punga anchor; joint.

pūngaiwerewere spider.

pūngao kōmaru solar power.

pungapunga anchor; yellow.

pungarehu ashes.

pungawere wind.

pūngāwerewere spider.
pūngene sleeping bag.
puoro music; sing; rumble.
pūoru music.
pūpū winkle, *Lunella smaragda, Zediloma aethios.*
pupuha blow or spout like a whale.
pupuhi (passive pūhia) to blow; to swell; to shoot.
pupuri (passive puritia, pupuritia) hold, retain.
pupuru stiff; thick.
pura blind; foreign matter in the eye; twinkle.
pūrahorua messenger sent for help.
pūrākau legend; myth; tale.
pūrama light bulb.
pūranga pile.
purapura seed.
pure ceremony for removing tapu.
pūrehu moth.
pūrēhua moth.
purei play.
pūremu adultery; to commit adultery.
purepure spotted; in patches.
pūrere engine; machine, machinery; motor.
pūrere horoi washing machine.
pūrere horoi maitai dishwasher.
pūrere whakaahua photocopier.
purini dessert, pudding.
pūriri New Zealand oak, *Vitex lucens.*
puritanga handle (noun).
pūrongo news; report.
pūrongo pēke bank statement.
purotu good-looking, handsome.
pūru bull.
purū blue.

puru cork; plug; cram in.
puruhi flea.
purūma broom; sweep.
purupuru to stop crevices of.
pūruru shady (of trees etc).
puta appear; be born; come out; hole, move onwards; opening; pass, pass through.
puta noa throughout.
pūtahi agency, centre; institute.
putaihu nostril.
pūtaiao science.
pūtake ancestor; base; cause; reason; root.
putanga appearance; exit.
pūtangitangi paradise shelduck, *Tadorna variegata.*
putaputa full of holes.
putaputawētā Māori may, *Carpodetus serratus.*
pūtātara shell trumpet.
pūtē basket.
pūtea bank account; basket; budget; finance; fund; funding; pocket; savings.
pūtea tāpiri subsidy.
pūtea taurewa loan.
pūteketeke crested grebe, *Podiceps cristatus.*
pūtere stranger.
pūtiki knot; to knot; topknot.
putiputi flower.
pūtohe saxophone.
pūtōrīno flute-like instrument.
pūtu boot; foot.
putu lie in a heap; store.
pūtumu slow-moving.
pūweru coarse flax cloak.
pūweto spotless crake, *Porzana tabuensis plumbea.*
pūwhā green vegetable, sow-thistle, *Sonchus oleraceus.*
pūwhara fighting stage of pa.

R

rā date; day; but; sail; sun; then; adverb indicating remoteness, over there, there, yonder.

rā whānau birthday.

rā ririki stars.

Rāapa Wednesday.

rae forehead; headland; temple.

raha open; extended.

rahi great; loud; many; welcome.

Rāhina Monday.

Rāhoroi Saturday.

raho testicles.

rahu basket made of undressed flax.

rāhui sign or mark of warning to trespassers, especially against infringement of tapu; ban; reserve; reservation.

rahurahu to handle; to interfere with.

rāia word giving emphasis.

raihana licence.

raihi rice.

rāina line.

raiona lion.

rāitarihā the day before yesterday.

raka agile; indicates position away from person spoken to, over there, there; lock.

rākai adorn.

rākau pole; stick; tree; wood; wooden.

raki dried up; north.

rakiraki duck.

Rakiura Stewart Island.

rako albino.

raku scrape; scratch.

rakuraku scrape; scratch; guitar; rake.

rama lamp, light (artificial); torch.

rama waka traffic lights.

ramarama shrub or small tree, *Lophomyrtus bullata*.

Rāmere Friday.

rānei serves the purpose of a question mark; either; or.

ranga group of people; perform rites over; raise.

rangapū company, group.

rangatahi fishing net; youth.

rangatira chief; noble; chiefly; boss, manager.

rangatiratanga control; dominion; evidence of greatness; freedom; kingdom; sovereignty.

rangi arrange in rows; heaven; period of time; day; period; sky; tune; weather.

rangimārie peaceful.

ranginamu handsome.

rangiora shrub, *Brachyglottis repanda*.

rangirua confused; uncertain.

rangitahi temporary.

rangitoto lava; scoria.

rango blowfly.

rangona heard (passive of rongo).

rāoa choked.

raorao plains.

rapa(-ia) to search, seek, look for.

raparapa ankle; projecting ends of the maihi or bargeboards

of a meeting house; sole of
the foot; to be in doubt; to
guess.
Rāpare Thursday.
raparere bastard.
rape tattooing on buttocks.
rāpea indeed.
rāpeti rabbit.
rāpihi rubbish.
rāpoi cluster; swarm.
rapu(-a) to search, seek, look
for.
rapunga a search.
rapurapu to be in doubt.
rarā roar; make a dull sound.
rara rib; shoal.
rarahi big, great (plural).
raranga plait; weave.
rārangi line; list; queue; row.
rārangi ingoa roll.
rārangi kai menu.
rārangi kupu vocabulary.
rārangi pātai questionnaire.
rārangi take agenda.
rārangi taputapu inventory.
rārangi tatari waiting list.
rārangi tono menu (computer).
rarata quiet, tame (plural).
rārauhe bracken fern, *Pteridium
aquilinum.*
rare lolly.
rarī disturbance; uproar.
raro beneath; bottom; north
(Māori refer to north as
down, and to south as up);
north wind; under; the
underworld.
Rarohenga the underworld.
raru(-a) disappointment; to be
encumbered; to be hindered;
trouble; in trouble.
raruraru trouble; problem.
rātā tree, rātā, *Metrosideros*

robusta; southern rātā,
M. umbellata.
rata divination; doctor; friendly;
quiet; seer; sharp; tame.
rata kararehe veterinarian.
rātaka diary.
Rātapu Sunday.
ratarata sharp.
rātau them; they (three or more
people).
rātō west.
ratonga service, services.
ratonga ahi fire service.
rātou them; they (three or more
people).
Rātū Tuesday.
rau blade; crowd; feather;
hundred; leaf; number.
rāua them, they (two people).
rauemi resource.
rauhuia bushy herb, *Linum
monogynum.*
rauika assembly; heap.
raukawa tree, *Pseudopanax
edgerleyi.*
Raukawa Moana Cook Strait.
raukoti disturb; meddle.
raukura feather; plume.
raumahara puzzled.
raumati summer.
raupā cracked; calloused.
raupani frying-pan.
raupapa flat ground; series.
raupatu conquer; conquest.
raupeka confusion; distress;
doubt.
raupō reed, bulrush, *Typha
muelleri.*
raurangi another time.
raurau divinatory rite.
raureka deceitful.
rauriki sow-thistle, *Sonchus*
species.

rauroha extended.
rauru satisfied.
rautahi childless man or woman.
rautangi perfume.
rautao leaves for wrapping food in oven; to wrap round with leaves.
rautau century.
rautupu thunderstorm.
rauuru hair.
rauwene object of criticism.
rawa advantage; finally; forms the comparative or superlative of adjectives, too, very; goods; property, wealth; purpose.
rawahanga mischievous.
rāwāhi bank; shore; side; the other side; overseas.
rawakore poor, destitute; homeless.
rāwaru blue cod, *Parapercis colias*.
rawe close; excellent; tight.
raweke busy; disturb; prepare; meddle with; mischievous.
rāwhara raffle.
rawhi basket; grasp; hold firmly.
rāwhiti east; sunshine.
rea murmur; to grow up (of plants).
reanga generation.
rearea leaves of the korau or wild turnip.
rehe expert; wrinkle.
rehea puzzles; thwarted.
reherehe buttocks.
rēhia pleasant; pleased; pleasure.
rehu dim; spray.
rehutai sea spray.

rei(-a) bosom; chest; ivory; jewel; leap; party of travellers; rush; treasured possession; tusk.
reia to be sought after; to be popular.
rēinga leap; leaping place.
Reipa Labour (political party).
reiputa ivory pendant.
reira that circumstance; that place or time mentioned before; frequently has the effect of 'then'.
reka sweet; delicious.
rekareka itchy; tickling.
rekereke heel.
rekoata record.
Rēkohu the Chatham Islands.
rēmana lemon.
rēme lamb.
remu lower end (of a garment).
remuremu plant, *Selliera radicans*.
rengarenga lily, *Anthropodium cirratum*; New Zealand spinach, *Tetragonia expansa*.
reo language; dialect; speech; tone; voice.
reo irirangi radio.
rēpata leopard.
repe lump on skin.
repe hūare pupuhi mumps.
reperepe buttocks; tattoo marks on buttocks.
repo swamp; cannon.
rera thigh.
rere(-a,-ngia) escape; fall; flee; flow; fly; go; hang; hurry; any passage through the air; be plentiful; rise; run; said; sail; stretched out; suddenly; waterfall.
rereangi hang-gliding.

rerekē different, odd, strange, unusual.

rerekētanga difference.

rerenga distant relatives; flight; fugitives; refugee; sentence (grammar); survivors.

rerenga ahi fire escape.

rerenga o Tamanuiterā solar system.

rērere run from one place to another.

rererere run from one place to another.

rerewhenua railway.

rēri rail.

reri ready.

reta letter.

rēti rent.

reti toboggan.

rētihi lettuce.

retihuka ski.

retireti a slide; to skate.

retireti hukarere skiing.

retiwai water-skiing.

rewa be elevated; float; mast; melt; start.

rewarangi pedestrian crossing.

rewarewa Māori honeysuckle, New Zealand honeysuckle, *Knightia excelsa*.

rēwera devil.

rewha eyebrows; eyelid; cross-eyed.

rewharewha epidemic; flu, influenza.

rīanga insurance.

rīhi dish; lease.

rikarika abashed; hesitating.

rīki leek.

riki small; onion.

rikiriki exceedingly.

rikoriko twilight.

rima five.

rimu red pine, *Dacrydium cupressinum*.

rimurehia sea grass, *Zostera* species.

rimurimu seaweed; moss.

rīnena linen.

rino twisted cord; iron (metal).

ringa arm; hand.

Ringatū a religion originated by Te Kooti which retained 'te ringa tū' – the upraised hand – of the Paimārire (or Hauhau) faith.

ringakuti fist.

ringaringa arm; hand; sleeve.

ringawera cook, kitchen hand.

rīngi ring.

ringi shower; to pour (liquids).

rio withered; wrinkled.

ripa furrow; ridge.

rīpeka cross; crucify.

rīpene cassette; ribbon; tape.

rīpene ataata videotape.

ripo deep pool; whirlpool.

rīpoata report.

riri (passive **rīria**) anger; battle; quarrel; angry, mad; bad-tempered.

ririki small (plural).

ririo withered; wrinkled.

riro became; gone; happen; be acquired, got, obtained; taken away.

riroriro grey warbler, *Gerygone igata*.

rita litre.

rite agreed to; arrange; completed; equal; fulfilled; like; indicates corresponding in condition; prepare; ready.

ritenga custom; habit; likeness.

rito middle shoot of a plant such as flax.

riu bilge of canoe; valley.
rīwai potato.
rīwai parai french fries.
rō in; inside.
rō whare indoors.
roa height; length; long; tall; great spotted kiwi, *Apteryx haastii*.
roanga continuation; delay.
rohe area; boundary; region, especially tribal region; zone.
rohea weary.
roherohe mark off by boundary; to separate.
rōhi rose.
rohi loaf.
rōhutu shrub or small tree, *Neomyrtus pedunculata*; shrub, *Lophomyrtus obcordata*.
rōia lawyer.
roimata tears.
roiroi dwarf.
rokiroki exhausted, used up; preserve.
roko as soon as; indicates extension or increase.
rokohanga found; reached; to be happened upon.
roma channel; current.
rona to bind.
rōnaki gliding easily; sloping.
ronarona strangle.
rongo (passive **rangona**) feel; hear; news; obey; peace; sense; smell; taste; fame.
rongoā cure; medicine; solution; treatment.
rongomatua big toe; thumb.
rongonui famous.
rongopuku overhear.
rōpā lodger; servant; slave; bachelor.

rōpere strawberry.
ropi body; figure; person.
rōpū gang; group; (political) party.
rōrā person of low birth; powerless; slave.
rore snare.
rorerore barbecue.
rori road.
rōria Jew's harp.
rorirori clumsy; silly; stammering.
roro brain; front end of whare; marrow.
roroa long (plural).
rorohiko computer.
rorohuri foolish.
roromi crush; squeeze.
rota lottery.
roto in, inside; lake; midst; swamp.
rotu send to sleep by magic; sleep-producing spell.
rou mamao remote control.
rourou small basket for holding cooked food.
rū earthquake; shake.
rua both; grave; hole; pit; storehouse; two.
ruahine old woman; priestess.
ruaki vomit.
ruaki moana seasick.
ruānuku magician; wise person; wizard.
ruarua few.
ruawiki fortnight.
ruha worn out.
rui(-a) scatter; shake; shake down; sow.
rūkahu lie; nonsense.
rukaruka completely; utterly.
ruku(-hia) dive; sink.

rukuruku dip or dive
  frequently; wrap up small.
rūma room.
rūma moe bedroom.
rūma noho living room, lounge.
rūma unuunu changing room.
rumaki dip, immerse;
  immersion; drown; bury; bow.
runa to secure; to steer.
runaruna pastime.
rūnanga assembly; council.
runga above; over; south
  (Māori refer to south as up
  and north as down); top; up.
rūpahu lie; nonsense.
rupe New Zealand pigeon,
  Hemiphaga novaeseelandiae.

rūpeke gathered together;
  denotes completion of action.
rura brandish.
ruranga guest; stranger.
rure scatter; shake.
rūri ruler; survey.
rūrū wave about; handshake.
ruru New Zealand owl or
  morepork, *Ninox
  novaeseelandiae*; take shelter.
rūruhi old woman.
ruruku band.
rūrūwai foolish.
rūtā bluster.
rūtawa grey hair.
rutu(-a) jolt; tackle; toss
  about.

T

Tā Sir.

tā the ... of (te ... ā) forming possessive (singular); bail; feather; form of address; net; paint; print; publish; stalk; supplies the place of the verb 'to have'; saves repetition of a noun; tattoo; breathe.

tā kōrua your (singular, addressed to two people).

tā koutou your (singular, addressed to three or more people).

tā mātou our (singular, their and my).

tā māua our (singular, his or her and my).

tā moko art of tattooing.

tā rātou their (singular, three or more people).

tā rāua their (singular, two people).

tā tātou our (singular, three or more people).

tā tāua our (singular, your and my).

tae(-a) arrive, reach; colour, dye; amount to, proceed to, up to.

tae atu ki as far as.

tae noa ki up until.

taea to be done; to be able.

tāepa hang down.

tāepaepatanga o te rangi, te place where the sky hangs down to the horizon.

taewa cold (adj); foreigner; potato.

tahā calabash.

taha besides; side.

taha oranga fitness.

tāhae rob, steal; stealthily; robber, thief; young man, fellow; filth.

tāhake young man.

tahaki shore (used by anyone actually on the water); to one side.

tahanga empty; moderately, slightly; naked.

tahataha steep bank.

tahatai seashore.

tahatika coastline.

tāhau leg; skin.

tāhau o te ringa forearm.

tahe flow; menstruation.

tāhei collar-bone; necklace; stripes.

tāheke descend, drop; steep; waterfall.

tāhere hang up; to snare; to spear.

tahi(-a) altogether; one; quite; single; smooth with an adze; sweep; then; together; unique.

tahirā the day before yesterday; the day after tomorrow.

tahirapa eraser, rubber.

tahitahi scrape; to clean (house).

tahora gather; open country.

tāhū ridge pole.

tahu burn; cook; husband, wife; light; lover; to heat.

tahua heap of food; sum of money, fund.

tāhuhu ridge pole.

tāhuhu kōrero history.
tāhuna beach; dry; sandbank.
tahupera false.
tahurangi fairy.
tahuri turn to, set to work; to turn around; turn over, to capsize.
tahuti hurriedly; to run away.
tahuti mai welcome.
tai coast; form of address; the other side; sea; tide.
tai āniwhaniwha tidal wave.
Tai Poutini West Coast (South Island).
Tai Rāwhiti East Coast.
Tai Tokerau Northland.
taiaha hardwood weapon about 1.5 metres long with pointed tongue at one end and a long flat narrow blade at the other.
taiākotikoti wear out.
taiao environment.
taiapo carry.
taiari crush; drive back.
taiaroa exhausted; tired; souvenir of dead or captured enemy brought to mourner in revenge.
taiatea afraid; nervous.
taiāwhio encircle.
taiepa fence; wall (freestanding).
taihoa soon.
taihoa! hang on!
taika tiger; horse.
taikākā heartwood.
tāikarehā the day before yesterday.
tāiki rib; wicker basket.
taikiri expresses distress.
tāiko black petrel, *Procellaria parkinsoni*.
tāima time.

taimaha heavy.
taimana diamond.
taimau betrothed; engaged.
tāina singe; toaster.
taina (plural **tāina**) junior; younger brother or cousin of a male; younger sister or cousin of a female.
tainahi the day before yesterday.
tāinakarehā the day before yesterday.
tāinanahi the day before yesterday.
tainui shrub, *Pomaderris apetala*.
tāingāwai place for baling out canoe.
taiohi young person, youth.
taiohinga youth (noun).
taipa be silent.
taipara fire a volley.
taipō goblin.
taipū heap; sandhill.
tairao linger; spend time.
taitāhae young man.
taitāhake young man.
taitai brush (verb).
taitama young man.
taitamāhine young woman.
taitamaiti child.
taitamariki youth.
tāitarihā the day before yesterday.
taitata near.
Tāite Thursday.
taitea pale; sapwood; white.
taitoa brave; manly.
taitonga south.
taitu slow.
taitua distant; the farther side; west.
taiwhanga ako classroom.

taiwhanga pūtaiao laboratory.
taiwharu gudgeon, *Galaxias brevipinnis.*
takā tie hook on line.
taka(-ina) come round (time); encircle; fall off; fall away; be formed, be developed; propose; turn; roam; roll; go round; on all sides; prepare; heap.
takaahuareka happy.
takahē South Island takahē, *Porphyrio hochstetteri*; North Island takahē, *P. mantelli* (extinct).
takahi(-a) stamp, trample; tread; disobey, violate.
takahore widow; widower.
takahorohoro impetuous.
tākai bind; wrap up; bandage.
takakau forearm; shin bone; stalk; straw; at leisure; unmarried.
tākakī neck; throat.
takakino act hurriedly; to abuse; to debase; to spoil.
takanewhanewha shut the eyes.
takapapa tablecloth.
takapau floor-mat.
takapau hora nui birth in wedlock.
tākapu Australasian gannet, *Morus serrator.*
takapū belly; calf of leg.
takāpui close, intimate.
takarangi faint; giddy; stagger.
tākaro play; presently; sport; wrestle; game.
tākaro ataata video game.
tākaro rorohiko computer game.
takatāpui close companion of the same sex; homosexual.

takatū prepare, get ready; set to work.
takawaenga mediator.
takawairore object of affection.
tāke tax.
tāke moni whiwhi income tax.
take beginning; cause; origin; reason; subject of discussion.
takeke garfish, *Hyporhamphus ihi.*
takere bottom (of sea, river etc); hull; keel.
taketake ancient; base (support); original, long-established, lasting; well-founded.
taki (prefix) so many at a time; e.g. takiono = six at a time.
taki to lead; to recite; to speak; to tow; to trace; challenge.
tākiri draw away quickly; untie; pull out; strike (as a match).
takirua in pairs.
takitahi individually.
takitaki appear; look for; provoke; recite; revenge.
takitaro moment.
takitini in droves.
takiwā area, district; period; time.
tako gums.
takoha pledge; token; tax.
takoki be sprained.
takonui big toe; thumb.
takoroa forefinger.
takoto(-ria) to be in position; to lie, to lie down; to lie before one in the future.
takotoranga position, site; receptacle.
tāku my (singular).
taku my (singular); border; edge.
takuahi fireplace.

takune pretend.

takunga an excuse.

tākupu Australasian gannet, *Morus serrator*; chief; twig, sprig.

takurua winter.

tākuta doctor.

takutai sea coast.

takutaku recite; threaten.

tama boy; man; son; eldest son.

tamāhine daughter; girl.

tamaiti child.

tamaiti whāngai adopted child.

Tāmaki-makau-rau Auckland.

tāmanga kōtore youngest child; youngest child but one.

tamariki children.

tāmaru shady.

tāmau betrothed.

tamawahine east.

tame heihei rooster.

tāmi press down; smother.

tāmiro(-tia) twist.

tamitami openly.

tamumu buzz; hum.

tāmure snapper, *Pagrus auratus*.

tāmutumutu intermittent.

tāna his; her; its (singular).

tana his; her; its (singular).

tāne bridegroom; husband; man.

tane ton; tonne.

tānekaha celery pine, *Phyllocladus trichomanoides*.

tāniko ornamental border of cloak, mat etc.

taniwha fabulous monster.

tanoni be sprained.

tanu(-mia) bury; plant.

tānumi fold in half.

tanumi behind; disappear.

tānga company.

tangai bark of tree.

tangata (plural **tāngata**) human; human being; man; person; slave.

tangata whenua host people or tribe; indigenous people; original inhabitants, people of the land.

tangatanga comfortable.

tangetange forthwith.

tangi(-hia) cry, weep; song of mourning; lamentation; funeral; mourn, grieve; reception (radio or television); sound; to make a sound.

tangihanga funeral; wake.

tangiweto cry; cry-baby.

tango(-hia) accept; acquire; attempt; receive; remove, subtract, take away; take; take hold of.

tango ake next; then.

tango atu next; then.

tango mai receive.

tangohanga betrothal, engagement; marriage.

tangoro blistered.

tangotango to handle; use.

tao to cook; spear (about two metres long); we two, us two (myself and the person addressed).

taokete brother-in-law (of a man); sister-in-law (of a woman).

tāone town; urban.

tāone nui city.

taonui flesh-footed shearwater, *Puffinus carneipes*.

taonga treasure; possessions; valuables.

taoroa long spear (about four to six metres).

tapa(-ia) cut; edge; margin; side; to name; to recite.
tapa tāone suburb.
tāpae present; to present; put before one.
tāpaepae jigsaw puzzle.
tapahi(-a) chop, crop, cut, slice; operate (perform surgery).
tapairu first-born female on whom rested a special tapu.
tāpapa stoop; lie face-down.
tapatapa groin.
tapatapahi cut in pieces.
tapawhā quadrilateral, rectangle.
tapawhā rite square.
tāpeka to wrap garment round oneself.
tapeke sum; the score; total.
tapepa stumble.
tāpi sticking plaster.
tāpiapia sticky.
tapiki double over; lay hold of.
tāpoa abscess.
tāpoi tourist.
tapoko enter; sink in mud.
tāpokopoko boggy.
tāpora to cook īnanga in baskets; baskets in which īnanga are cooked.
tāporepore faint, pass out.
tāpōrena raincoat.
tapou dejected; miserable.
tāpu bath, tub.
tapu forbidden; inaccessible; not to be defiled; sacred; under restriction.
tapuae footprint.
tapuhau calf of leg.
tapuhi nurse.
tāpui familiar spirits; set aside, reserve.

taputapu appliance; equipment; gadget; goods; incantation, spell; possessions; tool.
taputapu ā whare furniture.
taputapu rorohiko hardware (computer).
tapuwae footprint.
tāra dollar.
tara barb; black-fronted tern, *Sterna albostriata*; white-fronted tern, *S. striata*; clitoris; courage; peak; point; rough; spike; wall.
tarahae envy; quarrel.
tarahanga fork (of tree); saddle of hill; snare; trap.
tārai(-a) to shape or fashion (especially wood).
taraire tree, *Beilschmiedia tarairi*.
tara-iti fairy tern, *Sterna nereis*.
taraka truck.
tarakeha shriek.
tarakihana tractor.
tarakihi locust or cicada; a fish, *Nemadactylus macropterus*.
tarakitara tractor
tarakona dragon.
tara-nui Caspian tern, *Hydroprogne caspia*.
tarāoa bramble.
taranga shrub, *Pimelea longifolia*.
tarapakihiwi shoulder.
tarapeke jump.
tarāpunga red-billed gull, *Larus novaehollandiae*; black-billed gull, *L. bulleri*.
tarariki bitterly.
tararua with two points or peaks.
tarata lemonwood, *Pittosporum eugenioides*.

taratahi quarantine.
tarau trousers.
tarau poto shorts.
tarau tāngari jeans.
tārāuma chest; thorax.
taraute trout.
tarautete trousers.
tarawāhi side of bank, river, etc.
tarawhiti a ring.
tāre doll.
tārehu secretly.
tārekoreko grey.
tārera make faces (an act of defiance).
tārere natural swing (trailing vine in forest); to swing.
tārewa hanging, raised up; inconclusive; provisional; unpaid; unresolved.
tari bring; carry; government department; method of plaiting rope; office; study; urge.
tāria after a while.
taringa deaf; ear.
taro food plant, *Colocasia antiquorum*; bread; shortly.
taro ake in a little while.
taro kau iho in a very little while.
tārore snare; strangle.
tarotaro cut the hair.
tārū painful; shake.
taru grass; thing; vegetation.
taru kino drug; drugs.
tārua after a while; repeat.
tāruke avenge oneself; hurry; crayfish pot.
tārure become listless; suddenly.
tārūrū painful; shaking.
tātā contradict; criticise; smash down; stalk, stem.

tata close, near, nearby; nearly.
tātāeko whitehead, *Mohoua albicilla*.
tātahi seaside; wide apart.
tatanga nearness; ready.
tātai arrange; calculate; measure; line of descent; plan; recite genealogy.
tātaitai calculator.
tātaki kupu spelling.
tatangi tatau doorbell.
tatao younger brother; younger sister; deep; to droop.
tātāramoa bush lawyer, *Rubus cissoides*.
tātari analyse, review; sieve; sift.
tatari (passive **tāria**) to wait; to expect.
tātau we; us, (three or more people, including people addressed); everyone.
tatau to count; door; to push shutter; sliding door or shutter; to spell; to tie.
tātou we; us (three or more people, including people addressed); everyone.
tatauāoa casual acquaintance.
tatū agree; reach the bottom; be content; be resolved.
tatu stumble, trip.
tātua belt; girdle.
tātua tūru seatbelt.
tātuatanga put on clothes.
tāu your (singular, addressed to one person).
tau alight; be able; to bark; come to rest; float; interval of time; lover; neat, tidy; period; prepare to; reef; rest; expresses satisfaction; season; to sing; string; be suitable; year.

tau peke leap year.
tau toharite average.
tāua we two, us two, you and I;
female elder; grandmother.
taua army, war party; that
(before-mentioned).
tauapo hug.
tauera towel.
tauhanga arithmetic.
tauhinu scented shrub,
Pomaderris phylicifolia.
tauhou strange; stranger;
silvereye, *Zosterops lateralis*
(the bird was given this name
by the Māori because it was
not known in New Zealand
until the middle of the
nineteenth century).
tauihu bow of a canoe.
tauine ruler (stationery)
tauira copy; model; pattern;
teacher; wise person; student.
tauiwi foreign race; strange
tribe; New Zealanders of
European descent.
taukiri expresses distress,
surprise, etc.
taukumekume pull one against
another; debate.
taumaha heavy; weight;
serious, weighty.
taumaihi tower.
taumaka olive rockfish,
Acanthoclinus fuscus.
taumanu collar-bone; thwart of
canoe.
taumārō obstinate.
taumaru overshadowing;
shaded.
taumarumaru shady.
taumata brow of hill; resting
place on a hill; level; peak;
summit.

taumau betrothal; betroth;
betrothed, engaged; reserve
for oneself.
taunaha bespeak, reserve; lay
claim to.
taunga become accustomed to;
perch.
taunga ika fishing ground.
taunga wakarererangi airport.
tauomaoma race (athletics).
taupā fat covering intestines;
prevent.
taupaepae reception area.
tauparapara ritual chant,
usually at the beginning of a
speech.
taupatupatu to beat one
another; to compete with one
another; contradict; debate.
tāupe hunchback.
taupiripiri arm-in-arm; clasp
round waist.
taupoki to cover.
taupokina! attack!
taupū heap.
taupunipuni game of hide-and-
seek.
taura rope.
taura piu skipping rope.
tauraki drier; drought; to dry in
the sun.
tauranga anchorage; fishing
ground; resting place.
tauranga waka carpark.
taurangi changeable;
incomplete; wanderer.
taurapa stern-post of a
canoe.
taureka scoundrel; slave.
taurekareka scoundrel; slave.
taurepo shrub, *Rhabdothamnus
solandri*.
taurewa fugitive.

tauri band.
tauri kōmore wristlet or anklet of plaited fibre.
taurima entertain; hospitality.
taurima rererangi flight attendant.
taurite alike; opposite.
tāuru source; top (of tree etc).
taurua canoe used with large fishing net; double; doubt; even number; pair.
tautahi only child.
tautangata stranger.
tautara fishing rod.
tautau howl; to hang down.
tautauā coward.
tautauwhea person of low birth.
taute care for; look after; mourn; prepare.
tautika even, straight; level.
tautini for a long time.
tautohe contend; contest; persist; quarrel.
tautohetohe argue.
tautōhito adept; expert.
tautoko(-hia) support.
tautopenga goalkeeper.
tautuku bend.
taututeute jostle one another.
tauwaka numberplate.
tauwehe separate; to be separated.
tauwhāinga contend.
tauwhanga ambush.
tauwhare overhang.
tauwhena dwarf; small.
tauwherū tired.
tauwhiro care for, tend; social worker.
tawa tree, *Beilschmiedia tawa*; purple.
tāwaha entrance; opening.

tāwāhi the other side (of the sea, valley, river, lake, etc); overseas; international.
tāwai taunt; sneer.
tawaki Fiordland crested penguin, *Eudyptes pachyrhynchus*; Snares crested penguin, *E. robustus*.
tāwara murmur.
tāwari tree, *Ixerba brexioides*; exhausted; tired.
tawatawa blue mackerel, *Scomber australasicus*; paddle.
tawetawē noisy.
tāwhana curved.
tāwhaowhao driftwood.
tāwhara flower of the kiekie, *Freycinetia banksii*.
tāwharau be sheltered; shelter of branches.
tāwhe travel; turn corner.
tawhi toffee.
tāwheowheo New Zealand lilac, *Quintinia serrata*.
tāwhero tree, *Weinmannia silvicola*.
tāwheta writhe.
tawhitawhi delay; hesitate.
tāwhio go round about.
tāwhiri beckon.
tāwhiti trap.
tāwhiti whakaruatapu rat trap.
tawhiti distant; distance; generous; hospitable; person (used either admiringly or critically).
tawhito old.
tāwhiwhi tree, *Pittosporum tenuifolium*.
tē not; break wind.
te the (singular).
Te Ika a Māui North Island.

Te Moananui-a-Kiwa Pacific Ocean.

Te Moana o Raukawa Cook Strait.

Te Waipounamu South Island.

Te Whanganui-a-Tara Wellington.

tea clear; white.

tēhea? which? (singular).

teihana channel (TV); station.

teihana hinu petrol station.

teina (plural **tēina**) junior; younger brother or cousin of a male; younger sister or cousin of a female.

teitei high, tall, lofty.

teka dart (noun); lying; lie.

tekau ten (prior to the coming of the Pākehā, ngahuru was ten and tekau twenty).

tekau mā rua dozen.

teke vagina.

tekoteko carved figure on gable of whare; figurehead of canoe.

tēnā that there by you; this; here; there; but; each; encourage.

tēnā ko tēnei but on the other hand.

tēnā koe hello (to one person); thank you.

tēnā kōrua hello (to two people); thank you.

tēnā koutou hello (to three or more people); thank you.

tene impromptu.

tēnehi tennis.

tēnei any; each; here; now; this.

tēnei pō tonight.

tēnei rā today.

tēneti tent.

tenga Adam's apple.

tēpara stable.

tepetepe jellyfish.

tēpu table.

tēpu tuhituhi desk.

tērā that (far off); that other; he; she; then; there.

tērā marama last month; next month.

tērā tau last year; next year.

tērā wiki last week; next week.

tera saddle.

tere to drift; to float; party of travellers; swift, fast; swim (of fish).

terēina train.

tētahi a; each; one; some.

tētahi atu another.

tētahi mea something.

tētahi tangata someone.

tētahi wāhi somewhere.

tētē grey teal, *Anas gracilis*.

tetea gnash the teeth.

tētehi a; each; one; some.

tetere swollen.

tetetete chatter; rattle.

teti pea teddy bear.

tewe fermented tutu juice.

tewha working songs or chants.

tewhatewha long wooden axe-shaped club.

tēwhea? which? (singular).

tī cabbage tree, *Cordyline* species; tea.

tī hāte T-shirt.

tī kōuka cabbage tree, *Cordyline australis*.

tī rākau game in which sticks are thrown to and fro between players.

tia abdomen; adorn with feathers; stomach; passive termination.

tīaho shine.
tiakarete chocolate.
tiakete jacket.
tiaki(-na) guard, watch; care; care for, look after; maintain, preserve, protect, save.
tiāmu jam.
tīare scent.
tīeke saddleback, *Philesturnus carunculatus.*
tieke cheque.
tiemi see-saw.
tīere scent; jelly.
tīhae(-a) rip, tear.
tihe sneeze.
Tīhema December.
tīheru bale out water.
tihewa sneeze.
tīhi cheese.
tihi summit.
tīhore bald (an expression used jocularly, 'baldy'); bare; clear, clear up (of weather); peel; to strip.
tika correct, right; even; justice; reliable (of data); straight.
tīkākā burning; hot; sunburn.
tikanga culture; custom, habit, practice; meaning; method, way; purpose, reason; rule.
tikanga maha multicultural.
tikanga o te wā fashion.
tikanga rua bicultural.
tīkaokao fowl, hen.
tīkarohi scoop out.
tīkera kettle.
tiketike altitude, height; high; lofty; important.
tiki (passive **tīkina**) fetch; go; neck pendant, usually of greenstone, of stylised figure; carved figure of man on house.

tikihope loins.
tīkiti ticket, pass.
tīkitiki girdle; topknot.
tīkitiwhi detective.
tiko to defecate; excrement; to protrude.
tikoke high in the sky.
tī-kōuka cabbage tree, *Cordyline australis.*
tikumu hesitating; timid.
tīma team.
tima wooden grubber; streamer.
tīmata(-ria) start, begin.
tīmatanga beginning; origin.
tīmatatanga beginning; origin.
tīmere chimney.
timu ebb tide, shoulder; end.
timuaki top of the head.
tina dinner; lunch.
tinana body; in a mass; person; real; really.
tinei(-a) extinguish; put out.
tīni chain; change.
tini very many; horde (of people); tin.
tinihanga cheat; deceive; dishonest; improve.
tino has the effect of indicating the superlative degree, extremely, so, very; main; precise; real; self; special; reality.
tino pai very good; well done!
tino taonga valuable.
tino tau flash, impressive.
tino tika exact, precise.
tio oyster.
tīohu asthma, wheezing
tīpako select.
tīpakopako now and then, occasional.
tīpare chaplet, headband.
tīpāta teapot.

tipi glide; pare, slice.
tipiwhenua roam; vagabond.
tipu(-ria) genuine; to grow; own; a plant.
tipua demon; foreigner; giant; goblin; abnormal; genius; object of terror; steal.
tipuaki top of the head.
tipuna (plural **tīpuna**) ancestor; grandparent.
tipunga a plant.
tira rank; row; travellers; wand.
tira pūoru orchestra.
tīraha bundle; slow; lie face upwards.
tīrairaka North Island fantail, *Rhipidura fuliginosa placabilis*; South Island fantail, *R.f. fuliginosa.*
tīramaroa lighthouse.
tirara daffodil.
tīraumoko bastard.
tiriti street; treaty.
tīrehe faint, pass out.
tiro(-hia) look.
tiro mākutu stare.
tirohanga sight; view.
tirotiro examine, investigate.
tītaha lean or turn to one side; crooked; pass on one side; sideways; axe.
tītī sooty shearwater or muttonbird, *Puffinus griseus*; Cook's petrel, *Pterodroma cookii.*
tītī wainui fairy prion, *Pachyptila turtur.*
titi comb; insert; peg; pin; shine.
titihaoa shout of joy; shout with joy.
titiro (passive **tirohia**) to look; to check; to examine.

tītitipounamu rifleman, *Acanthisitta chloris.*
titiwai glow-worm, *Arachnocampa luminosa.*
tito compose story or song; fiction; invent.
tītoki New Zealand ash, *Alectryon excelsus.*
tītoko to keep away.
tītongi nibble.
tītore divide; split.
titorea make a slip-knot.
tiu north; north wind; soar.
tiutiu sparrow; thrush.
tīwaha shout for; shout after.
tīwai permanent; trunk of tree.
tīwaiwaka North Island fantail, *Rhipidura fuliginosa placabilis*; South Island fantail, *R.f. fuliginosa.*
tīwakawaka North Island fantail, *Rhipidura fuliginosa placabilis*; South Island fantail, *R.f. fuliginosa.*
tīwanawana fence; palisade.
tiwha mark; spot.
tīwhaiwhai wave about.
tīwharawhara stereo.
tiwhikete certificate.
tō(-ia) the … of (te … ō) forming possessive (singular), belonging to; as high as; dive; drag; open or shut; be conceived; pregnant; to set (of the sun); up to; used in place of the verb have; your.
tō kōrua your (singular, addressed to two people).
tō koutou your (singular, addressed to three or more people).
tō mātou our (singular, their and my).

tō māua our (singular, his or her and my).

tō rātou their (singular, three or more people).

tō rāua their (singular, two people).

tō tātou our, all of our (singular, three or more people).

tō tāua our (singular, your and my).

toa bravery, courage; champion, winner; hero; male (animal); romp; store, shop, dairy; warrior; win.

toa rongoā chemist.

toanga bravery.

tō-ā-papa gravity (force of).

toatoa tree, *Phyllocladus glaucus*; mountain toatoa, *P. aspleniifolius* var. *alpinus*.

toe be left, remain.

toenga left-overs; remainder; remnant.

toetoe grass, *Cortaderia toetoe*; sedge, *C. splendens*; shingle.

toha(-ina) allocate; distribute; spread abroad.

tōhau dew; sweat.

tōhē thief.

tohe(-a) argue; persist.

toheroa shellfish, *Amphidesma ventricosum*.

tōhi toast.

tohi divide, separate; ceremony for newborn baby.

tōhihi puddle.

tohitū direct; straight.

tohorā southern right whale, *Balaena glacialis*.

tohu(-ngia) award; badge; mark, sign; merciful; preserve; reserve; save; show, point out; tick.

tōhua yolk.

tohunga expert; priest; artist.

tohunga ahurewa high-class priest.

tohunga horomatua priest of third grade.

tohunga kēhua charlatan; imposter.

tohunga mākutu wizard.

tohunga matatuhi seer.

tohunga pouwhiro high-class priest.

tohunga ruānuku wizard.

tohunga tā moko one skilled in tattooing.

tohunga tūāhu high-class priest.

tohunga waihanga canoe-maker or carver.

tohunga whakairo master carver.

tohutaka recipe.

tohutō macron.

tohutoa medal.

tohutohu advise; guide; instruct; point out.

toi art; arts; finger; indigenous, native; tip; toe.

toihā pace to and fro.

toihau head.

tōihi stride.

toimaha heavy.

tōingo smart.

toiora healthy; spiritual welfare; uninjured.

tōiti little finger; little toe.

toitoi jog; jogging; trot.

toitū entire; permanent; undisturbed.

tōiwi good-for-nothing person.

toka rock.

tōkakawa sweat.

tokānuku important person.

toke worm.

toke hore tall person.
tōkena stocking; sock.
tokerau autumn; northern.
tōkere clappers, castanets.
toki adze; axe.
toko divorce (man and wife could have their union annulled by the repeating of certain karakia); pole; prefixed to some numerals and adjectives of number when describing people. When used it takes the place of the particle e.
tokoeka brown kiwi, *Apteryx australis.*
tokohana hiccup.
tōkohi adultery.
tokohia? how many people?
tokomaha many people.
tokomauri hiccup.
tokonui thumb; big toe.
tokotoko stick; walking-stick; weapon resembling quarterstaff.
tokouru west; west wind.
tokowhia? how many people?
tōku my (singular).
tōmairangi dew.
tōmato tomato.
tomo(-kia) begin; be filled; enter; pass in; pass out.
tomokanga entrance.
tōmua early.
tōmuri late.
tōna his, her (singular).
tonanawe loiter behind others.
tōnapi turnip.
tōneke trolley.
tōnihi move cautiously.
tono(-a) apply for; command; demand; invite; invitation; request; send away.

tonu always; continually; immediately; only; still; used to; used for emphasis.
tōnui thumb; big toe.
tōnga o te rā sunset.
tonga secret; south; south wind; suppressed.
tongi point; spot.
toparere helicopter.
tope(-a) cut down; cut off.
tōpito end; district.
tōpū double; couple; pair; assembled.
tōrangapū political; politics.
tōraro negative (number).
tōrea South Island pied oystercatcher, *Haematopus ostralegus*; pit for catching rats.
tōrea-pango variable oystercatcher, *Haematopus unicolor.*
toremi disappear; drowned.
torengi disappear.
tōrere abyss; desire.
tori cut.
tōrino basket; flute.
toro(-a) tree, *Myrsine salicina*; blaze, burn; discover; explore; extend; scout; a shoot; visit.
toroa wandering albatross (antipodean, Gibson's, snowy), *Diomedea* species; black-browed mollymawk, *Thalassarche melanophrys*; drawer.
toroa-haunui light-mantled sooty albatross, *Phoebetria palpebrata.*
toroa-whakaingo southern royal albatross, *Diomedea epomophora*; northern royal albatross, *D. sanfordi.*

torohē examine.
tōroherohe wag.
torohī diarrhoea.
torohīhihi short hair; few hairs.
torohū secret; secretly;
stealthily.
toroihi to bud, to sprout.
torōna throne.
toronga distant relatives.
toropapa shrub, *Alseuosmia
macrophylla* and *A.
quercifolia.*
tōrōpuku flesh.
torotika in a straight line.
torotoro hold out hands.
toru three.
tōrunga positive (number).
torutoru few.
tōtā sweat.
tōtahi almost; nearly.
tōtara tree, *Podocarpus totara*;
also used figuratively for a
chief or a canoe.
tote salt.
toti limp.
tōtika straight, directly.
tōtiti sausage.
tōtiti wera hot dog.
totō ooze, trickle.
toto bleed; blood.
totoa fierce; reckless; stormy.
totohe contend.
totohu to sink.
totoro stretch out.
totorore Antarctic prion,
Pachyptila desolata.
tōu your (singular, addressed to
one person).
tou buttocks, bottom; dip;
plant; set on fire.
touarangi rain.
toupiore lazy.
tourepa restless; wandering.

toutou dip into liquid; sprinkle
with water.
toutouwai New Zealand robin,
Petroica australis.
towene to set.
tū(-ria) to stand; to stop; to be
established; to rise or be high
(of waves); girdle; manner; to
remain; sort; to take place; to
be wounded; expresses a
moderate degree; erect.
tua back; cut down; distant
time; other side; this side;
spell used for different
purposes; time past.
tuahangata hero.
tuahine (plural **tuāhine**) female
cousin or sister of a male.
tuahiwi skeleton.
tūāhu sacred place used for
divination, altar.
tuaitara spines.
tuaiwi back; backbone.
tuakana (plural **tuākana**) elder
sibling or cousin of the same
sex; senior.
tūākari set (tennis).
tuaki(-na) disembowel, gut.
tuakiri identity; person.
tuakoka poor.
tuakoko backbone.
tuanui harsh; roof.
tūao working temporarily for
some other person.
tūāpae something bounding the
horizon.
tuarā back (noun).
tūāraki north wind.
tūārangi from far away;
ancient; important.
tuarea anxious; sorrowful.
tuarongo back wall of a
meeting house.

tuarua twice; repeat; second.
tuatahi once; first.
tuatangata hero.
tuatara reptile, *Sphenodon punctatus.*
tuatea anxious; pale.
tuatete hedgehog; reptile; rough, spiky; tuatara, *Sphenodon punctatus.*
tuatoru third.
tuatua chop up finely; main range; type of shellfish.
tūāua shower (rain).
tuauriuri very many.
tuawhenua mainland; inland.
tuawhiti fat; thick.
tuha to distribute; to spit, to spit out.
tūhangai bestride.
tūheihei untidy in appearance.
tuhi(-a) draw; glow; write.
tuhi ā ringa handwriting.
tuhinga essay; note; any piece of writing.
tuhituhi anuanu graffiti.
tūhourangi uncultured, rough.
tūhua obsidian.
tūhunga perch for birds.
tūī parson-bird, *Prosthemadera novaeseelandiae.*
tui(-a) to lace; pierce; sew; string on which anything is threaded; to thread.
tuiau flea; sandfly.
tūiri drill operated by cord.
tuitui(-a) fasten up; sew; cross lacing of decorative panel work.
tūkaha hasty; vigorous.
tūkari eager; lasciviousness.
tūkarikari handle roughly.
tūkawikawi eager; quick.
tuke elbow; jerk; knock; angle.

tūkeke lazy.
tukemata eyebrow.
tuketuke humerus ('funny bone'); incite; nudge.
tuki(-a) attack; pound; bunt (softball).
tūkino abuse, ill-treat, mistreat; wicked.
tukirakira dishevelled.
tukituki destroy, wreck.
tukorou desire; long for.
tuku(-a) allow; betray; to dye; let; let go; pass (sport); send, post; surrender.
tuku iho pass down.
tukunga person who welcomes guests.
tukutuku spider's web; decorative reed panels in meeting house.
tuma abscess.
tūmaeo lazy.
tumakuru fear.
tūmanako expect; hope; long for something not readily obtainable.
tūmāngai type of incantation.
tūmataiti private.
tumatakuru wild irishman, *Discaria toumatou.*
tūmatanui public.
tūmatarau covetous; mean.
tūmatatenga anxious.
tūmatohi watchful.
tūmau continuous, permanent; cook; servant; slave.
tume slow.
tumeke startled; frightened; awesome!
tūmere chimney.
tūmomo kind, type.
tumu cook; headland; stick; stump.

tumuaki crown of the head; head (of an organisation); president; principal.

tumutumu stump.

tuna eel.

tunewha sleepy.

tunu(-a) frighten; roast; bake.

tunuhuruhuru ill-treat a relative or friend; to offend.

tunutunu afraid.

tūnga position; wound.

tūnga pahi bus stop.

tunga toothache.

tungāne brother or male cousin of a female.

tungāne whakaangi step-brother of a female.

tūngaroa back portion of whare.

tungatunga beckon.

tūngoungou chrysalis of sphinx moth, *Agrius convolvuli*; larva.

tuoho bow; stoop.

tuoma run.

tuopu swap, trade.

tūoro kind of taniwha which lived underground.

tūpāpaku body, corpse; invalid.

tūpara double-barrelled gun.

tūpare shade eyes with hand; garland.

tūpato cautious, careful; suspicious; jealous.

tupehu angry.

tūpeka tobacco.

tūpeke high jump; jump.

tūpere pout.

tūpererū bluster.

tūpou headlong; stoop.

tupu(-ria) genuine; grow; own.

tupua demon; foreigner; giant; goblin; object of terror; abnormal; genius; steal.

tūpuhi storm; thin, lean.

tupuna (plural **tūpuna**) ancestor.

turaki(-na) overthrow; push down, subdue.

tūrama restless.

tūramoe sleepy.

tūranga foundation; tired; position.

Tūranga-nui-a-Kiwa Gisborne.

tūrangahakoa joy.

tūrangawaewae home place; spiritual home.

turapa to spring.

tūraparapa trampoline.

ture law.

tūrehu fairy (light-skinned, ghostly people who inhabit the forest); wink.

Tūrei Tuesday.

tureikura miserable.

tūrēiti late.

tūrere flee; run away.

turi deaf; knee; disobedient.

turihaka bandy-legged.

turikere deafened.

turingongengonge crippled; lame.

turipēpeke knees bent.

turipū weak in the knees.

turituri noise; threat.

turituri! be quiet!

turiwhatu slow.

tūroa of long standing.

tūrohi exhausted; tired.

turori stagger.

tūroro corpse; invalid; sick person, patient.

tūru chair, seat, stool.

turu last a little while; pole; post.

tūrua beautiful; middle.

tūruawe-pō middle of the night.

tūruhi tourist.
turuki crowded.
turuma latrine.
turuturu to make firm; leak; pole.
tuta back of the neck.
tūtae excrement; to excrete.
tūtai scout; sentry; spy.
tūtakarerewa apprehensive; unsettled.
tūtaki(-hia,-na) meet; meeting; shut.
tūtara gossip; slander.
tūtārere straggle.
tūtata near.
tūtaumaha spell, charm.
tute nudge; push.
tutetute jostle.
tūtira file; row.
tūtoko desire.
tūtoro dreamy.
tūtū summon.
tutū naughty; set on fire; stand erect; to be treated with violence; violent.
tutū te puehu expression for great disturbance, literally 'raise the dust'.
tutu small, poisonous tree, 'toot', *Coriaria arborea*; preserve birds in fat.

tūtūā person of low birth.
tūtuki (passive **tukia**) to bump, strike against; crash, collide.
tutuki to complete successfully, see something through; be achieved.
tūtukitanga crash, collison.
tutumaiao fabulous creatures of the seashore.
tūturi kneel.
tuturiwhatu New Zealand dotterel, *Charadrius obscurus*.
tūturu fundamental; natural; original; permanent; real.
tuturuatu shore plover, *Thinornis novaeseelandiae*.
tūtutupō glow; redness.
tūwaewae visitors.
tūwaharoa yawn.
tūwiri be afraid; terror; tremble; drill.
tuwha distribute; spit, spit out.
tūwhana urge.
tuwhara floor mat.
tuwhare saliva.
tuwheke afflicted with sores.
tuwhera open.
tūwhiti banish.

U

ū(-ngia) bite; breast; reach land, land; teat; udder; be firm, be fixed.

ua backbone; neck; rain; when.

uaki open or shut.

uakoao stranger (unaccustomed to present condition).

uara desire; value.

uarapa messy, untidy.

uarua raincoat.

uaua artery; difficult; firmness; muscle; strenuous; vein.

uauawhiti cramp.

ueke callous.

uepū company; party.

ueue disturb; incite; shake.

uha female (normally of animals).

uhi(-a) cover; tool used for tattooing, chisel; yam.

uho umbilical cord.

uhu stiffness.

uhumanea clever.

uhunga lament.

ui(-a) ask; enquire; question.

uira gleam; lightning.

uiui enquire for; to interview.

uiuitanga interview.

ūka cling tightly.

uka stop blood flowing.

ūkaipō mother (figurative).

uku wash; white clay.

ūkui rub, wipe.

ūkuikui rub, rub into; grind.

uma chest.

umanga business, occupation.

umere applause; shout.

umu earth oven; oven, stove.

unahi scale of fish.

unu(-hia) to take off (clothes); to drink.

ūnga place of arrival, landing place.

unga send.

ungaunga urge repeatedly.

upoko chapter; head.

upokororo grayling, *Prototroctes oxyrhynchus*.

uraura angry; flushed.

ure penis.

ure-tārewa male line of descent.

uri dark-green; descendant; race of humankind; relation.

Uropi Europe.

uru(-a) clump of trees; enter; hair; join; participate; west; west wind.

uru huarākau orchard.

uruao winter.

uruhau happy; pleased.

uruhi to drive; to force.

uruhua bruise.

uruhumu swelling.

urukehu fair-haired.

urunga pillow.

urungi rudder; steer; steering paddle.

uruora assistant; helper.

urupā burial ground, cemetery; come to an end.

urupounamu inquiry; question.

urupū diligent; preserving.

urupuia group of trees.

ururua overgrown; revelling.

urutā epidemic.

urutapu chaste; pure; virgin.

urutira dorsal fin.

uruumu swollen.
uruuru hasten; urge.
uruwehi be afraid; fear.
uruwhenua passport.
uruwhetū galaxy.
uta(-ina) inland; the land; to load.
utanga burden; freight; cargo.
utauta equipment; a load.
utiuti annoy; worry.

utu(-a) to pay; response, reply; revenge; cost, price; reward.
utu ā tau salary.
utu ā wiki weekly pay; pocket money.
uwha female (normally of animals).
uwhi(-a) to cover; covering; spread out; yam.
uwhiuwhi rain shower.

W

wā opportunity; period; region; season; time; while.

wā kāinga home.

wae foot; leg; separate.

waea to ring up, to call; telephone; be tired; wire.

waea pūkoro cellphone.

waea whakaahua facsimile, fax.

waehauā lame.

waenga middle.

waenganui middle.

waenganui pō midnight.

waengarahi middle.

waerenga clearing.

waero hair of dog's tail; tail.

waeroa mosquito.

waetea good runner.

waewae foot; footprint; leg; younger brother of a man.

waewae tapu stranger, newcomer.

waha broken; voice; carry on back; entrance; gate; mouth.

waha mautohe protestor.

wahahuka boasting.

wahakawa disliking ordinary food.

wāhanga period; season; section; channel (TV); term (school); chapter (book).

wāhanga whāomoomo intensive care unit.

wahangū dumb; quiet; silent.

wahapū entrance to harbour; eloquent; mouth of river.

waharoa gateway.

wahawaha approachable; genial; generous.

wāhi(-a) area; break; break through; part; piece; place.

wāhi tapu sacred place; cemetery.

wāhi utu checkout.

wāhi whakatau reception area.

wahie firewood.

wahine (plural wāhine) wife; woman; female; bride.

wahine mākutu witch.

wāhine murimanu lesser wives.

waho outside; open sea.

waho i te ture illegal.

wai liquid; memory; water; who?

wai āporo apple juice.

wai ārani orange juice.

wai petipeti jelly.

wai rēmana lemonade.

waia accustomed, used to; amuse; practise.

waiariki hot spring.

waiaruhe anguish; bitterness.

waiata(-tia) sing; song.

waiata ā ringa action song.

waihakihaki do; make.

waihanga(-tia) build; construct.

waihape to go about (of a ship).

waiho leave behind; let; let be; remain.

waihoki likewise, moreover.

waikamo tears.

waikauere worn out.

waikeri ditch.

waikorohuhō listless.

waikura rust.

waimaero weakened.

waimāori fresh water.

waimarie good omen; lucky, fortunate; quiet.

waimori lazy.
wāina wine.
waingāio unwelcome.
waingōhia easy; pleased.
waiora health.
waiora ā Tāne, te sunlight; the 'fountain of youth'.
waipiro alcohol, liquor.
waipounamu greenstone.
waipū volley of guns.
waipuke flood.
waipuna spring of water.
waipupuru yoghurt.
wairanu gravy; juice.
wairangi excited; infatuated; mad.
wairau bruised.
wairehi wireless, radio.
waireka contented; happy; soft drink, fizzy drink.
wairoro brains.
wairua spirit; soul.
Wairua Tapu Holy Ghost.
wairuhi listlessness; weakness.
waitahenga ditch.
waitai salt water.
waitakataka brains.
waitakiri twitch.
waitara hail.
waitau faint; immature; spiritless; worn out; timid.
waitaua army; expedition.
waitete dissension.
waitohu(-ngia) predict; mark, symbol, icon.
waiū milk (human).
waiwai to soak.
waka boat, ship, box; canoe; crew of canoe; receptacle, container; group of tribes (descendants of pioneers who came in a particular canoe); vehicle, car.

waka huia carved box for holding huia feathers and other small valuable articles.
waka para whenua bulldozer.
waka pēpi pram, pushchair.
waka rererangi aeroplane.
waka tinei ahi fire engine.
waka tūārangi spaceship.
waka tūroro ambulance.
waka whakatakere submarine.
wakahiki crane.
wakatere speedboat.
wakatono taxi.
wakawaka bed; row.
wakewake hurry.
wana bud, sprout; ray of light; thrill.
wānanga educational gathering, workshop; to hold in-depth discussions; Māori place of learning.
wananga threaten.
wanawana fear; fearsome; shiver; thrill.
wanea satisfaction; satisfied.
wani(-a) criticise; swan.
waoku jungle.
wāpu wharf.
wara desire; indistinctly; indistinct sound; murmur.
warahoe false.
waraki strange, uncommon.
warawara long for.
ware(-a) careless; ignorant; of low birth; thoughtless.
warea absorbed in, preoccupied; made unconscious.
wareware forgetful; forgotten; thoughtless; to forget.
waro abyss; burning coal; charcoal; pit.

waru(-hia) eight; scrape; shave; cut the hair.

wātaka timetable.

wātea vacant, free, unoccupied; cautious.

wati a watch.

wau discuss; quarrel; to be talked about; to be the subject of gossip.

wauwau grumble.

wāwā fence; palisade.

wawā scattered.

wawaenga average.

wawana fierce.

wawao defend.

wawaro murmur.

wawata daydream; desire.

wāwau discuss; quarrel; to be talked about; to be the subject of gossip.

wawe early; first; quickly; soon; too soon.

waweroka decided upon.

wē cry, squeak, squeal.

wehe(-a) detach; divide; leave; separate; enraptured.

wehenga departure; division.

weherua anxious; divided; midnight.

wehewehe arrange; to sort.

wehi to fear; terrible.

wehiwehi awe; regard.

weka woodhen, Gallirallus australis.

weku to scrape; to tear.

wene dislike; envy; grumble; many; sprout.

wenerau grumble at; the envy of many.

Wenerei Wednesday.

wenewene calabash; gourd, Lagenaria vulgaris; disagree; scab; scar.

wepu whip.

wera burn; heat; hot; warm.

werawera perspire; perspiration, sweat.

weriweri offensive, disgusting.

wero(-hia) challenge; dare; injection; pierce; sting; throw spear.

werowero stab frequently.

weru garment.

wētā insect, Hemideina crassidens; cave weta, Gymnoplectron edwardsii.

wete free; untie; refuse dare.

wetiweti disgusting.

weto cry; weep; to be extinguished; to put out (as of fire).

weu fibre; rootlet; single hair.

wewehe love-sick.

weweia New Zealand dabchick, Poliocephalus rufopectus.

wī game of tag.

wiki week.

wikitōria victory.

wini wind; window.

wīra wheel.

wira will.

wiri bore; drill; gimlet, auger; shiver; tremble; twist.

wiriwiri tremble.

witi wheat.

Wīwī France; French.

wīwī flinch; rushes of several species.

wiwini dread; terror.

wūru wool.

wuruhi wolf.

Wh

whā four.
whae form of address to woman, aunt, mother.
whaea aunt; mother, mum.
whāereere mother.
whai (passive **whāia**) to aim; cat's cradle; to play at cat's cradle; chase, follow, pursue; possess, have; perform ceremony; proceed to; short-tailed stingray, *Dasyatis brevicaudatus*; skate, *Raja australis*.
whai rawa rich, wealthy.
whai repo eagle ray, *Myliobatis tenuicaudatus*.
whai taonga rich, wealthy.
whaiāipo in love; darling, sweetheart.
whaiao daylight.
whaiaro person; self.
whaiawa river-bed.
whaiere express astonishment or disapproval.
whaihanga virtual reality.
whaihua useful, effective, worthwhile.
whaikōrero make a speech, especially on the marae ātea.
whāinga goal, objective; pursuit.
whāiti narrow.
whaitiri thunder.
whaiwhai chase, hunt.
whaiwhaikōrero hold a formal discussion.
whaka- towards; a common prefix which gives to an adjective or verb the sense of 'the act of', to a noun the form of a verb expressing the meaning 'like', or to an adjective, noun or verb it gives the sense of 'to cause to'. A number of meanings of words with this prefix follow; but the list is not exhaustive. In most cases the meaning of a word can be found from its alphabetical listing and the value of whaka- as a prefix added.
whakaae(-tia) consent; agree.
whakaaetanga agreement, permission.
whakaahua drawing; painting; photocopy; photograph; picture.
whakaahua kē disguise.
whakaako(-na) teach.
whakaangi float; hurl oneself; dive; indicates 'step' relationship.
whakaara enemy; enemy war party; raise; rouse; wake.
whakaari drama; to expose, to show; programme (TV); skit.
whakaariki invading army.
whakaaro(-hia,-ngia) consider; idea; intention; opinion; plan; purpose; think; thought.
whakaaroaro consider.
whakaarorangi turn towards.
whakaata reflection; look at reflection; reflect; mirror.
whakaata roto X-ray.
whakaatea clear away.

whakaatu(-ria) show, demonstrate; exhibit; to model.

whakaaturanga exhibition; publicity, promotions.

whakaaweawe lover.

whakaeaea lift from water.

whakaeke attack; enter; guest.

whakaemi to gather together, collect.

whakaero dwindle.

whakaeto dissolve; evaporate.

whakahaere(-tia) to direct; explore; lead; manage; to make to go.

whakaharahara extraordinary; great, highly important; huge.

whakahau to command.

whakahauhau command; encourage; song to encourage workers.

whakahauora refresh; revive.

whakahaupapa(-tia) freeze.

whakahāwea abuse, belittle; despise.

whakahē blame; condemn; disagree.

whakaheke ngaru surf, surfing.

whakaheke tupu to insult.

whakahekeheke striped.

whakahemo to consume; to be finished; to kill.

whakahere conciliatory gift; offering to gods.

whakahīhī arrogant; conceited; enterprising; to jeer; proud.

whakahina grandchildren (poetical).

whakahinuhinu glossy.

whakahipa head.

whakahira presume.

whakahirahira great, highly important; amazing.

whakahoa to be friendly with.

whakahoanga friendship.

whakahōhā annoy; bore.

whakahoki(-a) to answer; return; turn back.

whakahōnore to honour.

whakahora headlong.

whakahore deny; refuse; make of no account.

whakahori disbelieve.

whakahoro rākau training with weapons.

whakahoroa let down; slip off.

whakahua recite; quote; pronounce.

whakaihiihi exciting.

whakainu give drink to.

whakaingoa(-tia) name.

whakaingoingo sob.

whakaipo cherish; court.

whakairi(-a) hang up; raise.

whakairo carve; carving.

whakaiti belittle; despise; diminish; shrink; reduce; be humble.

whakakā switch; to turn on (switch).

whakakāhore deny, refuse; negate.

whakakāhoretanga negation.

whakakai earring.

whakakākahu to dress.

whakakakara to scent.

whakakaniwha barb; notch.

whakakapi to fill up a space; close.

whakakapōwai barb; notch.

whakakapi to fill up; replace, subsitute.

whakakapōwai to preserve human head.

whakakata funny, amusing.

whakakeke continue doing; refuse to speak.

whakakī to fill.

whakakikiwa eyes shut tightly.

whakakino treat with contempt, abuse.

whakakite display.

whakakoekoe tickle.

whakakoi sharpen.

whakakoia assent, agree.

whakakore abolish; cancel; delete; pass up; turn off.

whakakori tinana aerobics; physical exercise.

whakakorikori arouse; shake.

whakakoro instead.

whakakorokoro relax.

whakakotahi unite; unify.

whakamā ashamed; embarrassed; embarrassing; shy.

whakamahana to warm; heater.

whakamahara(-tia) to remind.

whakamahau porch; verandah.

whakamahi(-a) set to work; operate; use; utilise.

whakamaiangi type of incantation.

whakamaimoa to treat.

whakamāmā make easy, simplify.

whakamamae inflict pain; feel pain.

whakamana give effect to, authorise.

whakamanawa encourage; inspire confidence.

whakamania to scold, abuse verbally.

whakamanu transform into bird.

whakamāori(-tia) explain; interpret; translate into Māori.

whakamārama(-tia) explanation; explain.

whakamarara scatter.

whakamarie pacify.

whakamaroke to dry; cause to wither.

whakamarumaru to protect; to shade; to shelter.

whakamataku to scare.

whakamātau(-ria) make trial of; try; attempt; test.

whakamātauranga trial.

whakamātautau to attempt; test, exam; try on.

whakamate kill.

whakamau fasten; to fix, to set.

whakamaumaharatanga memorial.

whakamīharo surprising; wonderful.

whakamihi praise, acknowledge, thank.

whakamoe close eyes; put to sleep; give in marriage.

whakamoemiti praise, thank.

whakamōhio(-tia) inform.

whakamomori commit suicide; to fret, grieve.

whakamua forwards.

whakamuri backwards.

whakamutu finish, quit.

whakamutunga end; ending; finish; last; youngest child.

whakanamunamu look like a dot in the distance.

whakanoa make free from tapu.

whakanoho give in marriage; make to live or sit.

whakanui celebrate; enlarge; hang up; to make or consider important; to multiply.

whakangā rest.

whakangahau concert, show; amuse, entertain; encourage.
whakangahoro charge.
whakangaio dissemble, trick; pretend.
whakangaoko tickle.
whakangaro destroy; put away.
whakangau hunt with dogs; make to strike with weapons.
whakangāwari move quickly; ease, alleviate.
whakangita eye; face.
whakangote lactation; mammal; suckle.
whakaoho startle; wake up.
whakaomoomo nurse or look after a child or invalid.
whakaongaonga excite.
whakaora cure; rescue; save.
whakaoraora to excuse.
whakaoti(-a) to finish, complete.
whakaotinga finish; youngest child.
whakapae accuse; besiege; lay across; contend; estimate.
whakapahoho stationary.
whakapai approve; bless; praise; prepare; set in order.
whakapaipai decorate; make-up; ornament.
whakapaipaitanga decoration.
whakapākanga youngest child.
whakapakari strengthen, develop.
whakapākehā translate into English.
whakapakoko to dry (as of human heads in preservation process); image, hence statue, memorial; chief man of the tribe.

whakapapa genealogy; to lie flat.
whakaparahako despise; reject.
whakapātaritari provoke; toy with.
whakapati bribe.
whakapau consume, use up; exhaust; finish; pass time; spend.
whakapehapeha boast; conceited; pride; vain.
whakapīoioi to rock.
whakapiri(-a) fasten; stick (with glue).
whakapiro consider offensive.
whakapōauau drug (narcotic).
whakapono believe; faith; religion; trust in.
whakapoururu frown, look sad.
whakapū heap; stack.
whakapuaki to tell, disclose.
whakapuare to open.
whakapupuni hide oneself.
whakaputa publish; make come out.
whakaputu savings.
whakarae exposed; green; prominent; raw.
whakarākei theatre set.
whakarapa unlucky.
whakarāpopoto summary; summarise.
whakararu(-a) hinder; hindrance; to be occupied doing something.
whakarato pass round; serve.
whakarau capture; prisoner; multiply; slave.
whakaraupapa neutral.
whakarāwai to abuse; to sneer at.
whakarere(-a) forsake; to leave; suddenly; throughout.

whakarerekē to change.
whakarewarewa war-dance.
whakarihariha disgusted;
disgusting.
whakaripa along the edge.
whakarite(-a) appoint; arrange;
compare; decide; make like;
make ready.
whakaroa delay; hesitate;
lengthen.
whakarongo listen.
whakaruhi weaken.
whakaruruhau shelter;
protection.
whakarurutanga safety.
whakatā relax; rest.
whakataetae compete,
contend; competition,
contest; struggle.
whakataka assemble; deviate;
herd (noun); surround.
whakatakataka move about;
roll from side to side.
whakatakere bed of a river;
underwater.
whakataki recite; seek; lead
along; introduction, preface.
whakatakoto(-ria) lay down;
place; plan; set in place.
whakatanuku swallow.
whakatangi to make a sound;
to play (musical instrument).
whakatangitangi music.
whakatara to chaff; challenge;
defy.
whakatare eager.
whakatari incite.
whakatata approach.
whakatau(-a,-ria) to address;
decide; to mock; pretend; try;
visit; welcome.
whakatau tata estimate.
whakatau utu estimate, quote.

whakatauākī proverb.
whakataukī proverb.
whakataunga ā iwi
referendum.
whakatautau moan, wail.
whakatautopenga rearguard.
whakateka disbelieve.
whakatenetene annoy; quarrel.
whakatere buoy up; sail; steer.
whakatete gnash the teeth.
whakatika set off; straighten;
stand up; alter; fix; prepare.
whakatina confine; imprison;
seatbelt; starve.
whakatipi pass by; wanderer.
whakatipu(-ria) grow; bring up;
nurture.
whakatipuranga generation.
whakatō to plant; to father
child.
whakatohetohe unwilling.
whakatomonga cause to enter.
whakatoi annoy; cheeky,
impudent; tease.
whakatōkere perform ceremony
over bones of dead.
whakatōkihi move cautiously.
whakatopatopa give
commands; imperious.
whakatoro push forward;
reach; thrust.
whakatū(-ria) elect; erect;
establish; pass off; raise up; a
set speech; set up.
whakatuapeka pretend.
whakatuma anger.
whakatumatuma act defiantly.
whakatūpato to warn; warning.
whakatūpehupehu bluster;
rage.
whakatupu(-ria) grow; bring
up; nurture.
whakatupuranga generation.

whakaturi keepsake; love-token.
whakatutuki carry to completion.
whakatuturi to be obstinate; refuse to listen.
whakatuwhera to open.
whakatuwheratanga opening.
whakaū confirm; establish; support; surround.
whakauaua make difficult; strenuous.
whakaupa delay.
whakauru(-a) aid; ally; assist; avenger; import; insert; join.
whakaute care for; nurse.
whakautu(-a) caress; reply, respond.
whakauuwhi entertain.
whakawā accuse; condemn; to judge, appraise.
whakawaha to load; put load on back.
whakawai amuse; practise.
whakawaiwai amuse; practise.
whakawaireka to please.
whakawaitui to redden.
whakawarea distract; hinder.
whakawareware deceive.
whakawātea make way for, clear space.
whakawāwā quarrel; wrangle.
whakawehi protection.
whakaweti threaten.
whakawiri be anxious; tremble; twist; wring.
whakawiriwiri cruel; violent.
whakawhānau to give birth.
whakawhei cause people to quarrel.
whakawhēnanau strain.
whakawhere oppress.
whakawhetai thank.

whakawhetū wakeful.
whakawheua stand firm.
whakawhirinaki rely on, trust.
whakawhiti carry across; cross over; exchange.
whakawhiti kōrero communicate; exchange ideas.
whakawhiti whakaaro communicate; exchange ideas.
whakawhiu afflict; oppress; punish.
whakawhiwhi give; to award.
whāki confess; disclose.
whana company; kick; party; to rebel; rush; spring back.
whanake cabbage tree, *Cordyline australis*; to spring, grow.
whanaketanga youth.
whānako steal; theft; thief.
whananga party of travellers.
whānāriki sulphur.
whanatu go; go away.
whānau be born; family (in a broad sense); offspring.
whānau mārama children of light (sun, moon and stars).
whānau pani chief mourners, close kin of deceased.
whanaunga relative.
whanaungatanga kinship; relationship.
whanewhane liver.
whano behave; go; on the point of.
whanonga behaviour.
whanowhanoā feeling of annoyance.
whānui broad, wide; widely; width.

whanga bay; body of water; lie; lie in wait; stride; to measure.

whāngai(-a,-hia) feed, nourish; adopted; adopted child.

whanganga method of measuring by extending the arms to their full length.

whangō hoarse; inarticulate; nasal.

whāō devour; grab.

whaowhao to carve.

whaowhina fill; put in.

whara hit; be struck; to injure or be injured.

whārahi broad.

whārangi trees, *Brachyglottis repanda* and *Melicope ternata*; page of book.

wharau temporary shed.

whare building; house; shed.

whare haumanu clinic.

whare herehere prison.

whare hoko trading store.

whare iti toilet.

whare kairangi palace.

whare karakia church.

whare kawhe café.

whare kōhanga nest-house, house where baby was born.

whare kōpae house with door at side.

whare kurī kennel.

whare maire house for instruction in sacred lore.

whare mātā house for storing and preparing fowling implements, etc.

whare matoro house for social intercourse.

whare motokā garage.

whare pakimairo house of amusement.

whare pī beehive.

whare pikitia cinema, movie theatre.

whare pītakataka gymnasium.

whare pora house where weaving is done.

whare pōtae house of mourning.

whare pōuri jail, prison.

whare pukapuka library.

whare pūkiore house with elaborate reed decoration.

whare rēhia gymnasium; leisure centre; house of amusement.

whare rangi raised storehouse.

whare ropa house of amusement.

whare rūnanga meeting house.

whare taka meeting house.

whare takaha house for storing and preparing fowling implements, etc.

whare taonga museum.

whare tapere house of amusement; theatre.

whare tauā house for mourners (occupied while avenging party was absent).

whare toi art gallery.

whare tuhituhi study (noun).

whare tunu parāoa bakery.

whare wānanga traditional school of higher learning; university.

whare whakairo carved house.

whare witi barn.

whare whakanoho framed house made of wrought timbers.

whareiti toilet.

wharekai dining hall; restaurant.

wharekura house of learning; secondary school.

wharemoa hollow.

wharenui meeting house; hall.
wharepaku toilet.
wharepuni sleeping house.
whāriki(-hia) mat; spread out.
whārite(-a) compare; scales for weighing.
wharo abuse; scold.
whārona move quickly; run.
whāronatanga stride.
wharowharo spit.
whārua footprint; valley.
whāruarua concave.
whata platform, erected on wooden pole or poles, for storing food and keeping rats away; cupboard.
whata mātao refrigerator.
whata roa ā Manaia, te stomach.
whātai gaze.
whātero protrude (of the tongue).
whāti fudge.
whati(-a) broken, snapped; break, snap; run away; turn.
whatianga elbow.
whātinotino stretch out the neck.
whatinga flight.
whatitiri thunder.
whatitoka doorway.
whatiwhati break off; break into pieces.
whātōtō ancestor.
whatu eye; pupil (of eye); weave; knit; stone; hailstone.
whatukuhu kidney.
whatumanawa kidney; seat of feelings (used in the same sense as 'heart' by Pākehā).
whatungarongaro disappear.
whatupango pupil (of eye).
whaturei breast-bone.

whaturua very fat (of birds).
whātuturi to be obstinate.
whau tree, *Entelea aborescens*.
whaupa to overeat.
whaupaku five-finger, *Pseudopanax arboreus*.
whāura fierce.
whāuraura bluster.
whauwhau five-finger, *Pseudopanax arboreus*.
whāwhā feel; hold.
whāwhai hurry; impatient; urgent.
whawhai fight; scold; resist.
whawhaki to gather, pluck, pick.
whāwhāpū great pleasure.
whāwhārua hollow; female ancestor; mother.
whawhati break off; broken; chapped.
whawhe disturb.
whawhewhawhe busybody; meddler.
whē dwarf.
whea what place?; any place.
wheāngaanga undecided.
wheinu thirst; thirsty.
wheinga enemy; quarrel.
whēkau laughing owl, *Sceloglaux albifacies* (extinct).
wheke creak; octopus.
whēkere very dark.
wheketere factory.
whēkiki annoy; quarrel.
whēkite dazzled; see dimly; see for the first time; haze.
whēkoi move about.
whekoki crooked; wriggling.
whekowheko indistinct.
whena dwarf; firm.
whēnanau grunt.

whenua country; ground; land; afterbirth, placenta.
whengei quarrelsome; resentful.
whengu snort; blow (the nose).
whenguwhengu snuffle.
wheo hum; moan.
wheori ill; virus.
wheoro reverberate; rumble.
where oppress; overcome.
whererei protrude.
whero orange; red.
wheroku weaken.
wherori stagger.
whēru wipe (the bottom); toilet paper.
wherū mope; slow; tired; uncomfortable.
wheta dodge; struggle.
whētau dodge; wriggle.
whete stare wildly.
wheteke servant; wrinkled.
whetewhete whisper.
wheti full; rotund.
whetoko pace; step.
whetowheto insignificant; of low birth.
whetū star.
whetūrangi(-hia,-tia) appear in the heavens; die.
whētuki throb.
wheua bone.
whēuaua difficult.
whēwhē abscess; boil.
whewheia enemy.
whika arithmetic; figure.
whio blue duck, *Hymenolaimus malacorhynchus*; whistle.

whiore tail of an animal.
whira fiddle, violin
whiri(-a,-hia) plait; twist.
whirikoka strength.
Whiringa-ā-nuku October.
Whiringa-ā-rangi November.
whiriwhiri(-a,-hia) choose, decide, deliberate on.
whiro evil.
whiroia Antarctic prion, *Pachyptila desolata*.
whītau felt-tip pen.
whitawhita eager; quick.
whiti(-a) cross over; east; jump; recite; relate; shine; shock; start with alarm; verse, poem; hoop.
whitiāhua movie.
whitinga o te rā sunrise.
whītiki belt; to tie.
whito dwarf.
whītoki tie up.
whitu seven.
whiu(-a) gathered together; kill; place; prison sentence; punish; put; surfeited; throw, pass; together; turn; to whip.
whiuwhiu wag.
whiuwhiu para litter.
whiwhi(-a) acquire, get; own; possessed of.
whiwhiu take flight.
whoroa floor.
whurū flu (influenza).
whutupaoro football; rugby.

English – Māori

A

a he; tētahi, tētehi.
ability āhei; kaha.
able āhei, taea; kaha.
abnormal tipua, tupua.
abound hua.
about tata ki.
above runga.
abscess tuma.
absent hapa; ngaro.
abundant hua.
abuse kanga.
abyss tōrere.
accept tango.
accident aituā.
accommodating ngāwari.
accompany haere tahi i.
according to e ai ki.
accuse whakapae.
ache kōrangaranga; mamae; (headache) ānini.
achieve eke; tutuki.
acid kawa.
acknowledge mihi.
acre eka.
across (at right angles) hāngai; whakapae; (the other side) tua atu; (across valley, water) i/kei rāwāhi, tāwāhi.
act (deed) mahi.
action mahi.
action song waiata ā ringa.
active kakama; hihiko.

actor kaitapere.
add āpiti, hono; (mathematics) tāpiri.
address kāinga.
admire mīharo; mihi.
adult pakeke.
adultery pūremu.
advance, to paneke.
advantage huanga.
adventure pahī.
advertise pānui.
advertisement pānui.
advise tohutohu.
advocate kōkiri.
adze toki.
aerobics whakakori tinana.
aeroplane waka rererangi.
affect pā.
affection aroha.
affix, to whakamau.
afloat mānu.
afraid mataku; wehi.
Africa Awherika.
after āmuri, muri.
afternoon ahiahi.
afterwards muri iho.
again anō.
against ki.
age (years) tau; (childhood) pakeke.
agency pokapū, pūtahi.
agenda rārangi take.

agent māngai.
agree whakaae, tatū.
agreement whakaaetanga.
agriculture ahuwhenua.
aim whai; (purpose) take.
air hau.
airport taunga wakarererangi.
alarm (burglar) pahū.
alarm clock karaka whakaoho.
alas! auē!
albatross, light-mantled sooty
 toroa-haunui.
albatross, royal (southern,
 northern) toroa-whakaingo.
albatross, wandering
 (antipodean, Gibson's,
 snowy) toroa.
albino korako.
alcohol waipiro.
alight (get off) heke.
alike taurite; rite; ōrite.
alive ora.
all katoa.
alligator ngārara arikata.
allow tuku.
ally whakauru; hoa.
almost tata tonu ki; tata ki.
alone anake, anahe; kau.
along i.
already noa; kē.
also hoki.
alter (correct) whakatika;
 (change) whakarerekē.
although ahakoa.
altitude tiketike.
always i ngā wā katoa; tonu.
ambulance waka tūroro.
ambush haupapa.
amen amine.
America Amerika.
ammunition kariri.
among i roto i; waenganui i.
amuse whakawai; whakangahau.

amusement arcade wāhi
 whakangahau.
ancestor tupuna (plural tūpuna);
 tipuna (plural tīpuna).
anchor punga.
anchorage tauranga.
anchovy korowhawha.
ancient tawhito.
and me.
angel anahera.
anger riri.
angle koki.
angry riri, tupehu.
animal kararehe.
ankle pona.
anniversary huritau.
announce pānui.
announcement pānui.
annoy mukākā, utiuti,
 whakahōhā, whakatenetene,
 whakatoi, whēkiki.
another tētahi atu.
answer, to whakahoki,
 whakautu.
ant pokorua.
anxiety āwangawanga,
 māharahara, mānukanuka.
anxious āwangawanga,
 māharahara, mānukanuka.
any he; tētahi; ētahi (plural),
 tētehi, ētehi (plural).
anything aha.
appear puta.
appearance āhua.
appetite hiakai.
applause umere; pakipaki.
apple āporo.
apple juice wai āporo.
appliance taputapu.
apply for tono.
appoint whakarite.
approach whakatata.
approachable wahawaha.

April Āperira, Paengawhāwhā.
apron ārai.
arbor vitae, New Zealand
  kawaka.
argue tautohetohe.
arise maranga.
arithmetic tauhanga.
arm ringa.
army taua.
arrange whakarite.
arrive tae.
arrogant whakahīhī.
arrow kōpere.
art toi.
art gallery whare toi.
artist tohunga.
arts toi.
as hei; kei; me.
as if ānō.
as though ānō.
ascend kake.
ash, New Zealand tītoki.
ashamed whakamā.
ashes pungarehu.
aside ki tahaki.
ask pātai, ui.
assemble mene, huihui,
  whakataka.
assembly hui, huihuinga,
  rauika, rūnanga.

assist whakauru; āwhina.
assistant hoa; kaiāwhina, piki.
asthma huangō.
astronaut kaipōkai tūārangi.
at a; hei; i; kei; ki; ko.
athlete kaipara.
athletics kaipara.
atom ngota.
attack huaki.
attempt whakamātau.
Auckland Tāmaki-makau-rau.
August Ākuhata, Hereturikōkā.
aunt whaea.
Australia Ahitereiria.
authority mana, maru.
autumn ngahuru.
avenge ngaki.
average tau toharite;
  wawaenga.
avoid karo.
awake ara.
awaken whakaara.
award tohu.
away atu.
awe wehi.
awful wehi.
awkward pakepakehā.
axe toki.

B

baby piripoho; pōtiki; pēpe, pēpi.
babysitter kaitiaki.
bachelor takakau.
back tuarā.
backbone iwituararo.
backpack pāhi.
backwards kōmuri.
backwater muriwai.
bacon pēkana.
bad kino.
badge tohu.
bag pēke.
bail ehu.
bait maunu.
bake tuna.
bald pākira, moremore.
ball paoro, pōro.
ballet ori hīteke.
balloon poihau, pūangi.
ballpoint pen pene pura.
ban rāhui.
banana panana.
band (music) pēne, tira pūoru; (head) pare; (group) rōpū; (stripe) tāhei.
bandage tākai.
bank (river) parenga, paretai.
bank (savings) pēke.
bank account pūtea.
bank statement pūrongo pēke.
baptise iriiri.
bar paepae.
barb tara.
barbecue hūhuna, rorerore.
bare kau.
bark (of dog) au, auau; pahū.
bark (of tree) hiako, kiri.

barley pāre.
barn whare witi.
barracouta mangā.
barren pakoko.
barricade ārai.
barter hoko.
base pūtake, take, taketake.
basin peihana.
basket kete.
basketball pāhiketepōro.
bat (animal) pekapeka.
bat (sports) patu.
bath tāpu.
bathe kaukau.
bathroom whare kaukau.
battle pakanga.
bay whanga.
beach one; tātahi.
beak ngutu.
beam paepae.
bear, to mau.
beard pāhau.
beat patu.
beautiful ātaahua, rerehua; hūmārie, hūmārire.
because i te mea, nō te mea.
beckon pōwhiri, tāwhiri, tungatunga.
bed moenga.
bed (garden) moa.
bed (river) whakatakere.
bedroom rūma moe.
bee pī.
beef mīti kau.
beehive whare pī.
beer pia.
before mua.
beg īnoi.
begin tīmata.

beginning tīmatanga, tīmatatanga.
behave whano.
behaviour whano.
behind muri.
belief whakapono.
believe whakapono.
bell pere.
bellbird korimako.
belly kōpū; puku.
belonging to ā; nā; ō; nō.
below raro.
belt whītiki; tātua.
bend piko.
benefit hua, huanga, painga.
bent piko.
berry kākano.
beside i.
besides hāunga.
besiege whakapae.
best pai rawa; tino pai.
betray tuku.
betroth taumau.
better pai ake, pai atu.
between ki waenganui o.
bewildered pororaru, pōhēhē.
bewitch mākutu.
beyond ki tua atu i.
Bible Paipera.
bicycle paihikara.
biddy-biddy piripiri.
big nui (plural nunui); rahi (plural rarahi).
bilge riu.
bill kaute, nama; pire.
bind takai, hou.
bindweed pōhue.
bird manu.
bird-catching plant parapara.
birthday huritau, rā whānau.
biscuit pihikete.
bishop pīhopa.
bite ngau.

bitter kawa.
bittern, white-faced matuku-hūrepō.
black mangu; pango.
blackberry parakipere.
blackboard papa tuhituhi.
blame whakapae.
blanket paraikete.
blaze toro, mura.
bleary-eyed mata kōhore.
bleed toto.
blind matapō; kāpō; pura.
blister kōpūpū.
block poraka.
block up pani.
blood toto.
blow (noun) moto.
blow frequently puhipuhi.
blow, to pupuhi; (nose) whengu.
blue kahurangi, kikorangi, purū.
blue cod rāwaru.
blunt pūhuki.
board papa; poari.
boast whakapehapeha.
boat poti.
body tinana.
boil, a whēwhē.
boil, to kōhua.
bold māia.
bomb pahū, pōma.
bone kōiwi, wheua.
book pukapuka.
boorish tūhourangi.
boot pūtu.
border (frontier) rohe; (hem) taku, tāniko.
bore (drill) wiri; (annoy) whakahōhā.
bored hōhā.
boring hōhā.
born whānau.
bosom poho.

boss pāhi, rangatira.
both rua; rāua tahi.
bottle ipu, pounamu.
bottom (buttocks) papa; raro; (of sea, lake etc) takere.
bough manga.
boundary rohe.
bow (of canoe, ship) ihu, tauihu; (weapon) kōpere; (knot) koromāhanga.
bow, to koropiko, tuoho.
bowels manawa.
bowl kūmete.
box pāka, pouaka.
boy tama.
bracelet kōmore, poroporo.
bracken rarauhe.
brain roro.
bramble tātaramoa.
branch manga, peka.
brass parāhi.
brave manawanui.
bravery toa.
bread parāoa (from flour); rewena.
break pakaru.
break off whawhati.
break through wāhi.
breakfast parakuihi.
breast ū.
breath tā; ngā; hā.
breathe tā; ngā; hā.
breeze matangi.
bribe whakapati.
brick pereki.
bride wahine.
bridegroom tāne.
bridge arahanga, arawhata, piriti.
bridle paraire.
bright kanapu.
bring kawe, mau.
bristles huruhuru.

brittle papa noa.
broad whānui.
broadleaf puka.
broken pakaru.
broken off whati.
broom purūma, tahitahi.
brother tuakana (older, of a male, plural tuākana); teina, taina (younger of a male, plural tēina, tāina); tungāne (of a female).
brown pōuriuri, parauri, paraone.
bruise marū, uruhua.
bruised maru; uruhua.
brush, a paraehe.
brush, to taitai.
bubble mirumiru.
bubble up koropupū.
bucket pākete.
budget pūtea.
budgie kākāiti.
buggy paki.
build hanga, waihanga.
builder kaihanga.
building whare.
bull pūru.
bulldozer waka parawhenua.
bullet matā.
bumblebee pī rorohū.
bump rutu; tūtuki.
bunch pū.
bundle paihere.
burden utanga.
burglar alarm pahū.
burn tahu.
burnt wera.
burst pahū.
bury nehu, tanu.
bus pahi.
bus driver kaitaraiwa pahi.
bus stop tūnga pahi.
bush (forest) ngahere.

business mahi; kaipakihi,
   pakihi; umanga.
busy raruraru; warea.
but engari; otirā.
butter pata.
butterfish marari.
butterfly pēpepe.

buttock papa.
button pātene.
buy hoko.
buyer kaihoko.
buzz tamumu.
by e; i; nā.

C

cabbage kāpeti.
cabbage tree tī .kōuka.
café whare kawhe.
cage kōrapa.
cake keke.
calculate tātai
calculator tātaitai.
calendar maramataka.
calf (young cow) kāwhe; (leg muscle) tapuhau.
calico kareko.
call karanga.
calm marino, āio.
camera kāmera.
camp puni.
camping noho puni.
cancer mate pukupuku.
candle kānara.
cannon pūrepo.
canoe waka.
cap pōtae.
cape mata.
captain kaihautū, kāpene.
captivity herehere.
capture whakarau.
car motokā, motukā; waka.
card kāri.
care tiaki.
care for manaaki, tiaki, taurima, tauwhiro.
careful tūpato.
carefully tūpato; āta.
careless ware.
caress miri.
cargo utanga.
carpark tauranga waka.
carpenter kāmura.
carpet whāriki.
carrot kāreti; uhikaramea.

carry hari, kawe, mau, waha.
carry on back pīkau.
cart kāta.
cartoon pakiwaituhi.
cartridge kāriri.
carve whakairo, whaowhao.
case kēhi.
cash moni.
cash card kāri moni.
cassette rīpene.
castle pā hirahira.
cat naki, ngeru, poti, puihi, tori.
catch hopu.
caterpillar anuhe.
caught mau.
cauliflower kareparāoa.
cause kaupapa; take.
cautious tūpato.
cave ana.
cease mutu.
cedar, New Zealand kohekohe.
cellphone waea pūkoro.
cemetery urupā.
cent hēneti.
centimetre hēnimita.
centre (office) pokapū, pūtahi; (middle) waenganui.
century rautau.
cereal pata kai.
certainly āna; mārika.
certificate tiwhikete.
chain tīni.
chair tūru.
chairperson kaiwhakahaere, tumuaki.
challenge taki, wero.
champion toa.
change huri, kawe kē; whakawhiti.

changing room rūma unuunu.
channel (water) awa, hongere; (TV) hongere, teihana, wāhanga.
chapter upoko; wāhanga.
character āhua.
characteristics āhuatanga (plural).
charcoal rahu.
chase whaiwhai.
cheap ngāwari.
check titiro; whakarite.
checkout wāhi utu.
cheek pāpāringa.
cheese tīhi.
chemist kēmihi, toa rongoā.
cheque haki, tieke.
chest poho, uma.
chew komekome, ngaungau.
chick pīpī.
chicken heihei; pīkaokao.
chief ariki; rangatira.
child pōtiki; tamaiti.
childhood hokoitinga, itinga, ohinga, tamarikitanga, whanaketanga.
children tamariki.
chimney tūmere.
chin kauae, kauwae.
chips kotakota; maramara; (potato) maramara rīwai.
chocolate tiakarete.
choke rāoa.
choose kōwhiri, whiriwhiri.
Christ Karaiti.
Christmas Kirihimete.
church whare karakia.
cicada kihikihi.
cigarette hikareti.
circle porohita, porowhita.
circumference pae.
circus maninirau.
city tāone nui.

clap paki, pakipaki.
class (category) karangatanga, rōpū; (school) karaehe.
classroom taiwhanga ako.
claw maikuku.
clay oneuku.
clean mā.
clean, to horoi.
clear (understood) mārama; (transparent) tea.
clearing waerenga.
clearly mārama.
clematis puawānanga.
clerk karaka.
clever ihumanea, kakama, mōhio, pūkenga, uhumanea.
cliff pari.
climb kake, piki.
cling piri.
cling togehter pipiri.
clinic whare haumanu.
cloak kahu, kaitaka.
clock karaka.
close kati; (eyes) nenewha.
close to tata ki.
close together pine.
clothes kahu, kākahu, pūweru.
clothes drier tauraki hurihuri.
cloud ao; kapua.
clown hako.
clumsy hauā.
coal waro.
coast tahatika.
coat koti.
cockle pipi; huwai.
coffee kawhe.
coin moni.
cold anu, makariri, mātao.
cold, a taewa; rewharewha.
collect whakaemi.
collection kohinga, kohikohinga.
college kāreti.

colour tae.
comb heru.
come haere.
come out puta.
comfort oranga ngākau.
comfortable ahuru, tangatanga.
comic book pukapuka
pakiwaituhi.
command whakahau.
committee komiti.
common kitea noatia.
communicate whakawhiti
kōrero, whakawhiti
whakaaro.
communication
whakawhitiwhitinga kōrero.
compact disc (CD) kōpaepae
pūoru.
companion hoa.
company (of warriors)
hokowhitu; (of people) ope,
rōpū; (business) kamupene.
compare whakarite, whārite.
compassion aroha.
compel ā.
compete whakataetae;
tauwhāinga.
competition whakataetae.
competitor kaiwhakataetae.
complain amuamu; komekome.
complete tutuki; whakaoti.
completed oti; rite.
computer rorohiko.
computer game tākaro rorohiko.
concave are.
conceited whakahīhī.
concept ariā.
concerned āwangawanga.
condemn whakahē.
confess whāki.
confident whakamanawa.
confine whakatina.
confirm whakaū.

confused pōkaikaha, rangirua.
confusion raupeka.
conger eel ngoiro.
connection hononga.
conscience hinengaro.
consent whakaae.
consider whakaaroaro.
constable katipa.
constant pūmau.
contact lens arotahi.
container ipu.
contemptuous whakarawai.
contend whakataetae.
content tatū.
contents ngā mea o roto;
(book) ngā rārangi kōrero.
context horopaki.
continuation roanga.
continue honohono.
continuously hūrokuroku.
contract, a kirimana.
contract, to mānihi.
contradict tātā, taupatupatu.
convalescent mātūtū.
conversation kōrero.
convolvulus pōhue.
Cook Strait Raukawa Moana,
Te Moana o Raukawa.
cook, a kuki, tūmau.
cook, to tao; tunu.
cooked maoa.
cool mātaotao.
co-operate mahi tahi.
copper kapa.
coprosma karamu.
copy tauira.
cord pona.
cork puru.
corn kānga.
corner (of a house, room etc)
koko.
corner (of a road, path etc)
koki.

corpse tūpāpaku; koiwi.
correct tika.
cost utu.
costume kahu.
cough maremare.
council rūnanga.
count tatau.
country whenua.
couple rua; tokorua.
courage māia, tara, toa.
court, to whakaipo.
courtyard marae.
cousin (male, of a female) tungāne; (older) tuakana; (younger) taina, teina; kaihana.
cover hīpoki; popoki.
covering hīpoki; popoki.
cow kau.
coward tautauā.
cowardice tāwiri.
crab pāpaka.
cracked pātotoi.
crake, marsh koitāreke.
crake, spotless pūweto.
cramp parerori.
cramped kōpā.
crane wakahiki.
crash, a tūtukitanga.
crash, to tūtuki.
crayfish kōura.
crayon pia kano.
creak kongangi.
cream kirīmi.
create hanga.
credit card kāri nama.
creek manga.
creep ngōki.
creeper, brown pīpipi.
crevice kapiti.
crew of canoe waka.

cricket (sport) kirikiti; (insect) pihareinga.
criminal tangata hara.
cripple hauā.
criticise wani.
crocodile moko ngārara.
crooked hape.
cross rīpeka.
cross over whakawhiti.
crow, blue-wattled kōkako.
crow, orange-wattled kōkako.
crowd hono; hui.
crowded kikī, tūruki.
crown karauna.
crucify rīpeka.
cruel whakawiriwiri.
crumb kongakonga.
crumble horo.
crush roromi.
crushed marū.
cry (weep) tangi.
cry out auē.
cuckoo, long-tailed koekoeā.
cuckoo, shining pīpīwharauroa.
cuddle awhi, awiawhi.
cultivate ngaki.
cultivation ngakinga.
culture tikanga.
cup kapu.
cupboard kāpata, whata.
current ia.
curse kanga; mākutu.
curtain ārai.
curved tāwhana.
custom ritenga; tikanga.
customer kiritaki.
cut motu; tori.
cut down tua.
cut off kotipū.
cut out poka.
cut up haehae.

D

dabchick, New Zealand
weweia.
dad pāpā.
daffodil tirara.
dairy (shop) toa.
daisy parani.
damaged pakaru.
damp mākūkū, haukū.
dance haka; kanikani.
dancer kaikanikani.
danger mate.
dangerous mōrearea.
dare (challenge) wero.
daring māia.
dark pōuri.
dark, very hinapōuri.
dark colour pango.
darling kare, tau, whaiāipo.
dart (noun) pere.
dart, to kōkiri.
dash āki.
date (calendar) rā.
daughter tamāhine.
dawn pūao; ata hāpara.
day rā; rangi.
daylight awatea.
daytime ao.
dead mate.
deaf turi.
dear (special) aroha; (term of
address) kare; (expensive) nui
te utu.
death mate.
debate taukumekume;
taupatupatu.
debt nama.
decay pirau.
deceitful raureka; tinihanga.
deceive raureka; tinihanga.

December Hakihea, Tīhema.
decide whakarite, whakatau.
decorate whakapaipai.
decoration whakapaipaitanga.
decrease heke, iti haere.
deep hōhonu.
defeated hinga, mate.
defend wawao.
defy whakatara.
degree Celsius whakarautanga.
delay whakaroa.
delicious reka.
delighted āhuareka.
demand tono.
demon tipua, tupua.
dentist pou niho, rata niho.
deny whakakāhore.
depart haere, māiki, wehe.
descend heke.
descendant mokopuna; uri.
describe whakaahua.
desert, a pakihi.
desert, to whakarere.
deserted mahue.
desire hiahia; pīrangi.
desk tēpu tuhituhi.
despair aurere.
desperate pōnānā.
despise whakahāwea.
destroy whakangaro.
destroyed whakangaro.
detective kairapu hara,
tikitiwhi.
devil rēwera.
dew tōhau; tōmairangi.
diagram hoahoa.
diamond taimana.
diarrhoea torohī.
diary rātaka.

dictionary papakupu.
die mate, hemo, hinga.
died mate; hemo.
diet nohopuku.
difference rerekētanga.
different rerekē.
difficult uaua.
dig kari, keri.
dig up hauhake.
digger (machine) mīhini keri.
diligent urupū; pukumahi.
dim rehu.
diminish whakaiti.
dinghy poti paku.
dinner kai, tina.
dinosaur mokoweri, mokotuauri.
dip tou.
direct tohitū.
direction ahunga, aronga.
director kaiwhakahaere, tumuaki.
dirt paru.
dirty paru.
disagree wenewene, whakahē.
disappear torengi.
disappear behind tanumi.
disappeared ngaro.
disappointment pōuri.
disaster aituā, parekura.
disbelieve whakateka.
disc porotiti.
disciple ākonga.
disclose whāki.
discover kite.
discuss kōrero, kōrerorero, whakawhiti kōrero.
discussion kōrero.
disease mate.
disguise whakaahua kē.
disgusted anuanu.
disgusting anuanu, weriweri.
dish rīhi.

dishes rīhi.
dishevelled tūkirakira.
dishonest tinihanga.
disk (computer) kōpae.
dislike kaikiri.
disobedient turi.
display whakakite.
dissolve whakaeto.
dissolved memeha.
distance tawhiti, mamao.
distant tawhiti, mamao.
distorted ngahu.
distract whakaware.
distress āwangawanga, raupeka.
distressed āwangawanga, raupeka.
distribute toha, tuha, tuwha.
district rohe, takiwā.
disturb whawhe.
disturbance rarī.
ditch waikeri, awakeri.
dive ruku, tō.
diver kairuku.
divide wehe.
divination niu.
division (boundary) wehenga; (mathematics) whakawehe; (military) matua, whare; (part of whole) wāhanga.
divorce toko.
do mea, waihanga.
do not kaua.
doctor rata, tākuta.
dodge karo, whetau.
dog kurī.
doll tāre.
dollar tāra.
dolphin aihe.
dominion rangatiratanga.
done mahia, oti.
donkey kāihe.
door kūaha, kūwaha, tatau.

doorbell tatangi tatau.
dotterel, New Zealand tuturiwhatu.
double pū, taurua.
doubt mānukanuka, raupeka, taurua.
downwards iho.
doze kānewha.
dozen tekau mā rua.
drag kume, tō.
dragon tarakona.
dragonfly kapowai.
drain awakeri.
draw huahua, tā, tuhituhi.
draw out kume.
drawing, a whakaahua.
dread pāwerawera.
dream moemoeā.
dreamy tūtoro.
dress kākahu.
dress, to kākahu, whakakākahu.
dressing gown kahu tangatanga.
dried up pāpuni.
drift tere.
drill tūiri, tūwiri, wiri.
drink inu.

drip pata, patapata.
drive taraiwa.
driver kaitaraiwa.
driver's licence raihana kaitaraiwa.
droop tatao.
drop makere; patapata.
drought tauraki.
drown toremi, toromi.
drowned paremo.
drug (medicine) rongoa; (narcotic) taru kino.
drunken haurangi.
dry maroke.
dry, to pāina; whakamaroke.
duck rakiraki.
duck, blue whio.
duck, grey pārera; karakahia.
duck, paradise pūtangitangi.
dull pōuriuri.
dumb ngū, wahangū.
dung tūtae.
durable ora roa.
dusk kakarauri.
dust puehu.
dwarf whena, whito.
dye tae.
dye, to tuku.

E

each ia; tēnā.

eager hīkaka, kaikā.

ear taringa.

early (in the morning) moata; (not late) wawe.

earring whakakai.

earth oneone; whenua.

Earth, the Ao.

earthquake rū.

east rāwhiti.

Easter Aranga.

easy ngāwari; māmā.

easy-going ngāwari.

eat kai.

ebb timu.

echo paoro.

eddy ripo.

edge mata, tapa.

education mātauranga.

eel tuna.

effect ariā.

effective whaihua.

egg hēki, hua-manu.

eight waru.

either rānei.

elbow whatīanga.

elder kaumātua; pakeke.

elderly kaumātua.

elect whakatū.

election pōti.

electric hiko.

electricity hiko.

elephant arewhana.

elf patupaiarehe; tūrehu.

eloquent tau; pai.

email karere hiko.

embark eke.

embarrassed whakamā.

embarrassing whakamā.

embrace awhi.

emergency ohotata.

emotions ngā kare ā roto.

employee kaimahi.

employer kaitukumahi.

empty kau.

enclose hao.

encourage whakahau.

end mutunga.

ended mutu.

enemy hoariri, whewheia.

engaged (to be married) hapui, taimau, taumau.

engine pūkaha.

England Ingarangi.

English Ingarihi, Pākehā.

enjoy hākinakina; noho pai.

enjoyable ngahau, pārekareka.

enlarge whakanui.

enmity pukuriri.

enormous tino kaitā.

enough heoi, kāti; ka nui; rawe.

enquire pātai; ui.

entangle whiwhi.

enter hou, kuhu, tomo, uru.

entertain whakangahau.

entertaining ngahau.

entire katoa.

entrance kūaha, kūwaha, waha.

envelope kōpaki.

environment taiao.

envy harawene, pūhaehae.

epidemic urutā.

equal rite.

equipment taputapu.

eraser (stationery) muku.

error hapa.

escalator aramaiangi.

escape oma.
establish whakaū.
estimate whakapae, whakatau tata.
eternal ora tonu.
evaporate whakaeto.
even tautika, tika.
evening ahiahi.
eventually nāwai.
ever tonu.
every ia; katoa.
everything ngā mea katoa.
evil kino; whiro.
exact tino tika.
exactly! āna!
exam whakamātautau.
examine tirotiro, torohe.
excellence hiranga.
excellent hiranga, rawe.
except hāunga.
exchange whakawhiti.
excited ihi, wana.
exciting whakaihiihi.
excrement tiko, tūtae.
excrete tiko, tūtae.
excuse whakaoraora.
exercise korikori tinana.

exhausted māuiui; ngenge.
exit putanga.
expect tatari.
expel pana.
expensive nui te utu.
expert pūkenga; tautōhito; tohunga.
explain whakamārama.
explanation whakamārama, whakamāramatanga.
explode pahū.
explore whakahaere.
export hoko ki tai.
exposed pūare.
extend whakaroa.
extended whakaroa.
extinct mate ā moa, ngaro.
extinguish tinei.
extinguished pirau.
extort apo.
extraordinary korokē.
eye kanohi, karu, mata, whatu.
eyebrow tukemata.
eyelash kamonga.
eyelid rewha.

F

face kanohi, mata.
face to face kanohi ki te kanohi.
face towards anganui.
facsimile waea whakaahua.
fact mea.
factory wheketere.
faded hātea.
fail hē.
faint (indistinct) tōrikiriki; (swoon) hauaitu; (weak) hemo, maiangi, waitau.
fair kiritea.
fair-haired urukehu.
fairy patupaiarehe; tūrehu.
faith whakapono.
faithful pono.
falcon, New Zealand kārearea.
fall ānewa, hinga, taka.
fall away taka.
fall off taka.
false hē; horihori, tahupera.
fame rongo.
family whānau.
famine wā kaikore.
famous hau; rongonui.
fan kōwhiuwhiu; (music, sports etc) kaiwhaiwhai.
fantail pīwaiwaka, pīwakawaka, tīrairaka.
far away pāmamao, tawhiti.
farewell (said to those staying) hei konei rā; (said to those leaving) haere rā.
farm māra; pāmu.
farmer kaiahuwhenua.
farther ki kō atu.
fashion tikanga o te wā.
fast hohoro, tere.

fasten here; hōtiki; kati; whakamau.
fat (grease) hinu; (large) mōmona.
father matua (plural mātua), matua tāne; pāpā.
father-in-law hunarei, hungarei.
fault hē.
favourite makau.
fax waea whakaahua.
fear wehi; mataku.
feast hākari.
feather huru, rau; raukura.
February Huitanguru, Pēpuere.
fed up hōhā.
feeble ngoikore.
feed whāngai.
feel, to whāwhā.
feeling ariā.
feelings ngākau.
feet waewae.
fellow tāhae, nauhea.
felt-tip pen whītau.
female uha, uwha; wahine.
fence taiepa.
fern, common hard piupiu.
fernbird matatā.
fern-root aruhe.
fertile mōmona.
fetch tiki.
fever kiri kā; piwa.
few itiiti, ruarua, torutoru.
fibre kaka, weu.
field māra; pārae, pātiki.
fierce wawana.
fight whawhai; pakanga.
figure hoahoa; whika.
fill whakakī.

fin pakikau.
finance pūtea.
find kite.
fine (of weather) paki.
finger korokoro, matimati.
fingernail matikuku.
finish whakaoti.
finished mutu.
fire ahi.
fire engine waka tinei ahi.
fire escape rerenga ahi.
fire fighter kaipatu ahi.
fire service ratonga ahi.
firewood wahie.
fireworks pahū ahi.
firm (company) kamupene; mārō; taketake; turuturu; ū; whena.
first tuatahi.
fish ika.
fish, to (with hook and line) hī; (with net) hao.
fisher kaihī.
fish-hook matau.
fishing rod matira, tautara.
fist meke, ringakuti.
fit (healthy) hauora.
fitness hauora.
five rima.
five-finger (tree) puahou, whauwhau.
fix whakatika.
fixed (immobile) mau.
flag haki, kara.
flame mura.
flash kōwhā, muramura; (of lightning) hiko, kohiko; (impressive) tino tau.
flat pāraharaha.
flat land papa.
flavour hā, kakara.
flax harakeke; korari.
flax fibre muka.

flea puruhi, tuiau.
flesh kiko.
flexible ngāwari, ngore.
flight rerenga; whatinga.
flight attendant taurima rererangi.
flint matā.
float tere.
flock pōkai.
flood waipuke.
floor kaupapa; papa; whoroa.
floppy disk kōpae.
flounder, sand pātiki.
flour parāoa.
flow rere.
flow freely pātere.
flower pua, puāwai, putiputi.
flu whurū.
flute kōauau; pū; pūtōrino.
flutter kakapa.
fly (noun) ngaro; rango.
fly back hūpana.
fly up hūpana.
fly, to rere.
flying-fish maroro.
foam huka.
focus arotahi.
fog kohu.
fold koru.
follow whai.
fond mateoha.
food kai.
fool hākawa.
foolish rorohuri.
foot waewae.
football hutupōro, whutupaoro.
footprint tapuae, tapuwae.
for hei; hoki; ki; mā; mō.
forbidden tapu.
force (noun) kaha.
force, to uruhi.
ford kauranga.
forehead rae.

foreigner rāwaho; tauiwi; tipua, tupua.
forest ngahere, ngāherehere; wao.
forever ake ake ake; mō ake tonu atu.
forget wareware.
forgive muru.
forgotten wareware.
fork mārau, paoka.
fork of tree tarahanga.
form āhua.
fort pā.
fortnight ruawiki.
found kite; rokohanga.
foundation tūranga.
fountain puna.
four whā.
fowl heihei.
fragment kongakonga, ngota.
fragrance angi, kakara.
framework anga.
fraud tinihanga.
freckle ira, iraira.
free (no cost) utukore; (vacant) wātea.
freedom rangatiratanga.
freeze whakahaupapa.
freezer pākatio.
french fries maramara rīwai.
fresh hou; māori.
Friday Paraire, Rāmere.
fridge whata mātao.

friend hoa.
friendly atawhai; rata.
friendship whakahoanga.
frighten whakamataku.
frightened mataku, wehi.
frog pepeke.
from i; nō; ō; mai i.
front aro; aroaro; mua.
frost huka; hukapapa.
frostfish para.
frown, a poururu.
frown, to whakapoururu.
fruit hua.
fry parai.
frying-pan parai, raupani.
fuchsia fruit konini.
fuchsia tree kōtukutuku.
fudge whāti.
fugitive rerenga.
full kī; kikī; mākona.
full stop kopi.
fun hākinakina; rekareka.
fund pūtea, tahua.
fungus hākeke.
funny (amusing) hangarau, whakakatakata; (peculiar) hangarau, rerekē.
furious pukuriri.
furniture taputapu ā whare.
furrow awa; huripoki.
further ki kō atu.
future āmua.

G

gadget taputapu.
galaxy ikarangi, uruwhetū.
gale āwhā.
game kēmu, tākaro.
gang rōpū.
gannet, Australasian tākapu, tākupu.
garage karāti, whare motokā.
garden māra.
garfish takeke.
garland tūpare.
garlic kanekane, kāriki.
garment pakikau.
gasp kuha.
gate kēti; putanga; (of a marae) waharoa.
gather kohi; whakaemi; whakahui.
gather into heap awha.
gathered together mine.
gauge ine.
genealogy whakapapa.
generation reanga, whakatipuranga, whakatupuranga.
generosity ohaoha; wahawaha.
generous ohaoha; wahawaha.
genius tipua, tupua.
gentle māhū.
gentleman rangatira.
gently āta.
genuine tipu, tupu.
germ iroriki.
get riro; tae; whiwhi.
geyser waiariki.
ghost kēhua.
giant tino nui; tipua, tupua.
giddy āmiomio.
gift koha; maioha.

gills piha.
gimlet wiri.
giraffe hīrawhe.
girdle tātua.
girl hine; kōtiro; tamāhine.
give (away from the speaker) hoatu; (towards the speaker) homai; whakawhiwhi.
glad hari koa.
glass karaehe.
glasses (spectacles) mōhiti, mōwhiti.
gleam uira.
gleaming kānapanapa.
glide tere.
gloomy pōuriuri, pōururu.
glory korōria.
glossy whakahinuhinu.
glow hinātore.
glow-worm titiwai.
glue kāpia.
gnaw ngau.
go haere; whano.
goal (objective) whāinga.
goal (sport) paneke.
goalkeeper tautopenga.
goat nanekoti, nanenane.
gobble apuapu.
goblin taipō.
god atua.
godwit, eastern bar-tailed kūaka.
gold kōura.
goldfish morihana.
golf hau paoro, korōwha.
gone haere; riro; wehe.
good pai (plural papai); ka pai!
good afternoon kia ora.
good health! kia ora!

good morning ata mārie, mōrena; kia ora.
goodbye (said to those leaving) haere rā; (said to those staying) e noho rā.
goodnight pō mārie.
goods taonga.
goose kuihi.
gooseberry kuihipere.
gorge kapiti.
gorilla kōriha, makinui.
gospel rongopai.
gossip tūtara.
gourd hue, ipu, tahā.
govern whakahaere tikanga.
government kawanatanga.
grab whao.
graffiti anuanu; tuhituhi.
gram karāmu, koma.
grandchild mokopuna.
grandfather koro; koroua, pōua.
grandmother kui; kuia, tāua.
grandparent tipuna (plural tīpuna); tupuna (plural tūpuna).
grape karēpe, kerepe.
grapefruit hua hīmoemoe.
grapevine aka wāina.
grasp rawhi; apo.
grass karaihe; otaota; pātītī; tarutaru.
grasshopper māwhitiwhiti.
grave (for burial) rua; (serious) taimaha, taumaha.
gravel kirikiri.
gravity (force of) kume-ā-papa, tō-ā-papa.
gravy wairanu.
grayling upokororo.
graze hārau.
great nui (plural nunui).

grebe, crested pūteketeke.
greedy kaihoro.
green kākāriki.
green, dark kānapanapa.
greenstone pounamu.
greet mihi.
grey tārekoreko.
grieve konohi; tangi.
grind huri; oro.
grindstone hōanga.
groan ngunguru.
groove awaawa.
groper hāpuku.
ground whenua.
group rōpū.
grove motu, uru rākau.
grow whakatupu; whanake.
grub huhu.
grumble komekome, wauwau.
guard dog kurī tautiaki.
guard, a tautiaki.
guard, to tiaki.
gudgeon taiwharu.
guess raparapa, rapurapu.
guest manuhiri.
guide dog kurī ārahi.
guide, a kaiārahi.
guide, to ārahi; arataki.
guinea pig poaka kini.
guitar rakuraku.
gull, black-backed karoro.
gull, black-billed tarāpunga.
gull, red-billed akiaki; tarāpunga.
gun pū.
gurnard, red kumukumu.
gush hīrere.
gust apu.
gymnasium whare pītakataka, whare rēhia.
gymnastics pītakataka.

H

habit tikanga.
hail ua whatu, waitara.
hailstone whatu.
hair huru; makawe.
hairdresser kaikuti makawe.
hair-root weu.
hairy pūhuruhuru.
half haurua, hāwhe.
hall hōro; wharenui.
hamburger hāmipēka, pākī.
hammer hama.
hand ringa.
handbag kete; pāhi.
handkerchief aikiha.
handle kakau.
handshake harirū.
handsome purotu, ranginamu.
handwriting tuhi ā ringa.
hang down tāepa, tautau.
hang up whakairi.
hang-gliding rereangi.
happen riro.
happy koa.
harbour whanga.
hard (difficult) pakeke, uaua; (not soft) mārō.
hardware (computer) taputapu rorohiko.
harm kino.
harrier, Australasian kāhu.
harvest ngahuru.
hasten uruuru.
hastily patiko.
hat pōtae.
hate mauāhara.
hawk, bush (New Zealand falcon) kārearea.
hawk, sea (brown skua) hākoakoa.

hay hei.
haze whēkite.
hazy kōrehurehu; kōtuhi; māhinahina.
he ia.
head māhunga; mātenga; pane; upoko.
headache ānini, ngāhoahoa.
headland mata, rae.
headline kupu matua.
headphones kawe rongo.
heal, to whakamāhū.
healed māhū.
health hauora, waiora; ora.
healthy hauora, toiora, ora.
heap ahu, haupū, pū, pūkai, pūkei, taka.
heap up peti, apo.
hear rongo.
hearing aid pārongo.
heart manawa; ngākau (figurative).
heart attack manawa hē, mate manawa.
heat wera.
heat, to whakawera.
heater whakamahana.
heatwave hīrangi, pakapaka.
heaven rangi.
heavy taimaha, taumaha.
hebe koromiko.
hectare heketā.
hedgehog hetiheti, tuatete.
heel rekereke.
height roa, tāroaroa, tiketike.
helicopter toparere.
hello kia ora; tēnā koe (to one person); tēnā kōrua (to two

people); tēnā koutou (to three or more people).

helmet pōtae mārō.

help āwhina.

helper kaiāwhina, piki.

hemisphere kōpae.

hen heihei.

her ia (pronoun); tāna, tana, tōna (singular possessive); āna, ana, ōna (plural possessive).

herb otaota.

herd whakataka; kāhui.

here konei.

here! anei!

hereafter anamata.

hero toa, tuahangata, tuatangata.

heron, reef matuku-moana.

heron, white kōtuku.

heron, white-faced matuku-moana.

herring (yelloweye mullet) aua.

hesitate tawhitawhi, tikumu.

hesitating tawhitawhi, tikumu.

hiccup tokohana.

hidden huna, whakapeke.

hide huna, whakapeke.

high ike, teitei, tiketike.

high jump tūpeke.

high school kura tuarua; wharekura.

high up paratū.

highway huarahi.

hijack kahaki.

hill hiwi; puke.

him ia.

hinder whakawarea.

hindrance whakararu.

hip himu; hope.

hippopotamus hipohipo.

his tāna, tana, tōna (singular); āna, ana, ōna (plural).

hiss hū.

history hītori; tāhuhu kōrero.

hit patu.

hitchhiker pakituri.

hoarse whango.

hockey hake.

hold pupuri.

hole kōrua; poka; puare.

holiday hararei.

hollow kohukohu.

home kāinga.

homesick manatu.

homework mahi kāinga.

homosexual takatāpui.

honest pono.

honey honi, mīere.

honeysuckle, Māori (New Zealand honeysuckle) rewarewa.

honour hōnore.

hoof matikuku.

hook matau.

hoop whiti.

hope tūmanako.

horizon pae.

horn hāona.

horse hōiho.

hospitable manaaki.

hospital hōhipera.

hospitality manaaki, manaakitanga.

hostage mau herehere.

hot wera.

hot dog tōtiti wera.

hot-air balloon pūangi.

hotel hōtera; pāparakāuta.

hour hāora.

house whare.

housework mahi ā whare.

how pēhea, pēwhea.

however heoi, heoi anō.

howl auau, tautau.

hug awhi, tauapo.

huge tino nui.
hull takere.
hum wheo.
human tangata; uri.
human being tangata.
humble whakaiti.
hunchback hake.
hundred rau.

hunger hiakai; pīkoko; matekai.
hungry hiakai; pīkoko; matekai.
hunt whaiwhai.
hurry whāwhai.
hurt mamae; whakamamae.
husband hoa tāne, tāne.
hymn hīmene.

I

I au, ahau; māku, mōku; nāku, nōku.
ice hukapapa.
iceberg motuhuka.
ice-cream aihikirīmi.
ice-plant horokaka.
icing huka.
idea ariā; kaupapa; whakaaro.
identical ōrite.
identity tuakiri.
idiot pōrangi.
idle makuku, māngere.
if ki; mā; me, mehemea, menā.
ignorant ware.
ill mate; māuiui; wheori.
illegal waho i te ture.
illness mate.
image āhua.
imagine pohewa.
immature waitau.
immediately ināia tonu nei, inamata.
immerse rumaki.
impact ariā.
impatient takakino, whāwhai.
impetuous takahorohoro.
import hoko ki uta; whakauru.
importance hiranga
important hira; mātua; matua; nui; taumaha; tiketike; whai tikanga.
impossible e kore e taea, kāore e taea.
impressive tino tau.
imprison hopu ki te herehere.
improve whakapai.
in hei; kei; ki; nō.
incantation karakia.
inch īnihi.

incite akiaki, tuketuke.
including tae atu ki.
income moni whiwhi.
income tax tāke moni whiwhi.
incomplete taurangi.
inconclusive tārewa.
increase oha; whakanui.
indeed! āe!; āe mārika!; āna!
independent motuhake.
indicate tohutohu.
indistinctly wara.
indoors roto.
industrious houhere, pukumahi.
infection mate.
influence awe; mana.
influenza rewharewha, tarutawhiti.
inform whakamōhio.
inhabit noho.
inject wero.
injection wero.
injure tūkino.
injury kino.
ink iniki.
inland uta.
innocent (naīve) kūare; (not guilty) harakore.
inquire pātai; uiui.
inquiry patapatai; urupounamu.
insect mata; mū; ngārara.
insert titi.
inside roto.
instead of tē.
instigate whakatū.
institute pūtahi.
instruct tohutohu.
insult mūheni.
insurance inihua, rīanga.

intelligent ihumanea, uhumanea; mātau; mōhio.
intend whakakoro.
intensive care unit wāhanga whāomoomo.
intercept hautoki; haukoti.
international o te ao.
internet ipurangi.
interpret whakamāori; whakamārama.
interpreter kaiwhakamāori; kaiwhakamārama.
interrupt aruaru.
interview uiuitanga.
intestines piro; puku.
into ki; ki roto ki.

invade whakaeke.
invalid (sick person) maki.
invent tene; tito.
inventory rārangi taputapu.
invisible ngaro.
invite pōwhiri; tono.
iron (for pressing clothes) haeana.
iron (metal) maitai.
irritable mānehenehe.
island motu; moutere.
it ia (not used as a rule of inanimate objects – the noun is usually repeated).
itch mangeo; māeneene.
its ana (plural); tana (singular).

J

jacket tiakete.
jail whare herehere.
jam tiāmu.
January Hānuere, Kohitātea.
jar haka; pounamu; tiaka.
jaw kauae, kauwae.
jealous hae, wene.
jealousy pūhaehae.
jeans tarau tāngari.
jeer whakahīhī.
jelly tiere, wai petipeti.
jellyfish tepetepe.
jerk nape.
jersey poraka.
Jesus Ihu.
jet lag ngenge rererangi.
Jew's harp rōria.
jewel rei.
jewellery kahurangi; rei.
jigsaw puzzle tāpaepae.
job mahi.
jogging hūrokuroku, toitoi.

join āpiti; hono; tūhono.
joint monamona.
joke hangarau.
journalist kairīpoata.
journey haere; haerenga.
joy hari.
joyride haerenga pokanoa.
judge kaiwhakawā.
judge, to whakawā.
judo nonoke.
juice wai; wairanu.
July Hōngongoi, Hūrae.
jump peke; tūpeke.
jumper poraka.
June Hune, Pipiri.
jungle waoku.
junior taina, teina.
junk otaota.
just kātahi tonu; kātahi anō;
   noa, noa iho.
justice tika.

K

kākā's beak kōwhai ngutu-kākā.
kangaroo kangaru.
karate karate.
kayak kōreti.
keel takere.
keen hiahia; kaikaha; ngākaunui.
keep pupuri; tiaki.
keepsake oha.
kennel whare kurī.
kettle tīkera.
key kī.
kick whana.
kidnap kahaki.
kidney whatumanawa.
kill kōhuru; patu.
kilogram kirokarāmu.
kilometre kiromita.
kind (nice) atawhai; ngāwari.
kind (type) momo, tū, tūmomo.
kindergarten kura kōhungahunga.
kindle hika.

king kīngi.
kingdom rangatiratanga.
kingfish haku.
kingfisher, New Zealand kōtare.
kiss kihi.
kitchen kāuta (cooking shed); kīhini, kītini.
kite manu; manu aute; manu tukutuku.
kitten punua poti.
knee pona, turi.
kneel tūturi.
knife māripi, naihi.
knit whatu.
knock tuke.
knot pona.
know mōhio.
knowledge mōhiotanga.
knuckle pona.
koala koara.
kowhai, red kōwhai ngutu-kākā.

L

laboratory taiwhanga pūtaiao.
labour mahi.
Labour (political party) Reipa.
lace, to kāpui.
lacebark houhere.
ladder arahanga, arawhata.
lady wahine.
ladybird pāpapa kōpure.
lake moana; roto.
lamb rēme.
lame hauā.
lament apakura.
lamp rama.
lamprey piharau.
lancewood horoeka.
land whenua.
landslide horo.
language reo.
large nui (plural nunui).
last whakamutunga.
late tōmuri.
later āmuri; āmuri ake nei.
laugh kata.
launch, to kārewa.
laurel, New Zealand karaka.
lavatory whare iti, wharepaku.
law ture.
lawyer poutoko ture, rōia.
lay down whakatakoto.
lay, to panga.
layer papanga.
lazy māngere, tūkeke.
lead (metal) matā.
lead, to ārahi.
leaf rau.
leak turuturu.
lean (thin) tūpuhi.
lean over hinga.
leap mawhiti.

leap year tau peke.
learn ako.
learner ākonga.
lease rīhi.
leash here.
leather kirikau.
leatherjacket (fish) kōkiri.
leave whakarere.
leek rīki.
left maui.
left, to be mahue.
leg waewae.
legend pakiwaitara.
lemon rēmana.
lemonade wai rēmana.
lemonwood tarata.
length roa.
lengthen whakaroa.
lens arotahi.
leopard rēpata.
less iti iho.
lesson akoranga.
lest kei.
let kia; tuku; waiho.
letter pukapuka; reta.
letterbox pouaka reta.
lettuce arata; rētihi.
level tautika; taumata.
library whare pukapuka.
licence raihana.
lick mitimiti.
lid kōpani; popoki.
lie (down) takoto.
lie (tell lies) teka; tito; rūkahu,
    rūpahu.
life ora.
lift hāpai.
light (natural) mārama;
    (artificial) rama.

light (not heavy) māmā.
lightbulb pūrama.
lighthouse tīramaroa.
lightning hiko; uira.
like kei; me; rite.
like that pēnā; pērā.
like this pēnei.
like, to aroha; pai.
likeness ritenga.
lilac, New Zealand
  tāwheowheo.
lime kota.
limestone pakeho.
limp toti.
line (row) rāina, rārangi;
  (fishing) aho.
line aho.
linen rīnena.
ling hokarari.
linger karioi, tairoa.
link hononga.
lion raiona.
lip ngutu.
lipstick pani ngutu.
liquid wai.
liquor waipiro.
list rārangi.
listen whakarongo.
listless ānewa.
litre rita.
litter parahanga, otaota.
litter, to whiuwhiu para.
little iti, nohinohi, paku.
live (at a place) noho.
live, to ora.
liver ate.

living room rūma noho.
lizard moko.
load pīkau.
load, to uta.
loaf rohi.
loan pūtea taurewa.
lobster kōura.
local ā rohe.
lock raka.
locust tarakihi.
lofty teitei, tiketike.
lonely mokemoke.
long roa (plural roroa).
long for hihiri.
look tiro, titiro.
look after tiaki.
look at mātaki, mātakitaki.
look for kimi, rapu.
look! nanā!
loop kopeti.
loose mātangatanga.
lost mahue; ngaro.
lots maha; nui; tini; (of people)
  tokomaha.
lottery rota.
loud hoihoi, rahi, turituri.
louse kutu.
love aroha.
lover tau, tahu, whaiāipo.
low hakahaka.
lucky waimarie.
lullaby oriori.
lunch tina.
lungs pukapuka.
luxury tino hāneanea.

M

machine mīhini, pūrere.
machinery mīhini, pūrere.
mackerel, blue tawatawa.
mad pōrangi.
magazine maheni.
maggot iro, kutukutu.
magic mākutu.
magician ruānuku.
magnet aukume.
magnify whakanui.
mail mēra.
main mātāmua; matua; tino.
mainland tuawhenua; uta.
maintain tiaki.
make hanga.
make-up whakapaipai.
male tāne; (of animals) toa.
mammal whakangote.
man tāne.
manage whakahaere.
manager kaiwhakahaere.
mango mango.
mangrove mānawa.
manners whanonga.
manure wairākau.
many huhua; maha; nui; wene.
many, very tūāuriuri.
map mapi.
marathon oma taumano.
March Māehe, Poutūterangi.
margarine patahinu.
margin tapa.
mark tiwha.
marriage mārenatanga,
    tangohanga.
marrow roro.
marry moe; mārena.
mast rewa; tira.
master māhita.

mat whāriki.
matagouri tūmatakuru.
match māti.
mathematics pāngarau.
matter (importance) hira;
    (problem) raruraru;
    (situation) take;
    (substance) mea.
mattress moenga.
maximum mutunga rawa.
May Haratua, Mei.
may, Māori punawētā.
maybe pea.
me ahau, au.
meal kai.
mean (stingy) matapiko,
    tūmatarau.
meaning tikanga.
measles karawaka, mītara.
measure ine; tātai; tīeke.
meat kiko; mīti.
mechanic kaiaka mīhini.
medal tohutoa.
media, the hunga pāpāho.
medicine rongoā.
meek māhaki.
meet tūtaki.
melon merengi.
melt rere; rewa.
member mema.
member of parliament mema
    pāremata.
memory mahara.
mend hanga; tapi.
menu (computer) rārangi tono;
    (food) rārangi kai.
merciful tohu aroha.
merry-go-round porowhawhe.
mess paruparu.

message karere; kupu; pānui.
messenger karere.
messy pōrohe, uarapa.
metal konganuku, mētara.
meteor kōtiri, kōtiritiri.
meter ine.
method tikanga.
metre mita.
microphone hopuoro.
microscope karu whakarahi.
microwave ngaruiti.
midday poupoutanga o te rā.
middle waenga, waenganui.
midnight waenganui pō,
  weherua pō.
might ekene; pea; tērā.
migrate heke.
migration hekenga;
  maunutanga.
mild māhaki.
mile maero.
milk miraka; waiū.
milkman kaituku miraka.
millilitre miririta.
millimetre mirimita.
millionaire mirionea.
mind (noun) hinengaro;
  ngākau.
mine nāku, nōku.
minibus pahi iti.
minimum iti.
minister minita.
minute meneti.
miracle merekara.
mirror whakaata.
mischievous rawahanga.
miserable tāpou.
miss (young lady) mihi.
miss, to hapa.
missionary mihinare,
  mihingare.
mist kohu, pokekohu.
mistake hapa; hara; hē; hori.

mistaken pōhēhē.
mister mita.
mistreat tūkino.
mix pokepoke.
moan wheo.
mock whakatau.
model (noun) tauira; (fashion)
  kaiwhakaatu.
model, to (fashion) whakaatu.
modern hou.
modest pōrearea.
mollymawk, black-browed
  toroa.
moment takitaro.
Monday Mane, Rāhina.
money moni.
monkey makimaki.
monster ngārara; taniwha.
month kaupeka, marama.
mood āhua ngākau.
moon marama.
moonlight atarau; ata marama;
  ata māhina.
mope wherū.
more nui ake, nui atu; rahi ake,
  rahi atu.
morepork ruru.
morning ata.
mosquito naeroa, waeroa.
moss rimurimu.
most (the majority) nuinga;
  (the greatest quantity) tino.
motel mōtēra.
moth pēpepe.
mother hākui; kōkā; kokora (of
  true mother only); matua
  wahine; whaea.
mother-in-law hunarei,
  hungarei.
motor mīhini, pūrere.
motor racing whakataetae
  motokā.
motorbike motopāika.

mountain maunga.
mountain bike paihikara maunga.
mountaineering pīkaunga.
mourn tangi; taute.
mouse kiore.
mouth māngai, waha.
mouth (of river, etc) pūaha, pūwaha, wahapū.
move kori; neke; nuku.
move about kānekeneke, whēkoi.
move along nuku.
move aside kotiti.
move onwards puta, whanake.
move quickly whakangāwari.
move slightly ngaoko.
movie pikitia, whitiāhua.
much nui.
mud paru.
muesli patahua.
mug maka.
mullet, grey kanae.
multicultural tikanga maha.
multimedia pāpāho maha.

multiply whakanui.
mum māmā; whaea.
mumps repe hūare pupuhi.
murder kōhuru.
murderer kaikōhuru.
murmur wara.
muscle io; uaua.
museum whare taonga.
mushroom harore.
music whakatangitangi; puoro, pūoru.
musician kaiwhakatangitangi.
mussel kuku, kūtai.
must mātua.
mustard panikakā.
mutilate mutumutu.
mutter hameme; hāmumumumu.
mutton mīti hipi.
muttonbird ōi, tītī.
my taku, tāku, tōku (singular); aku, āku, ōku (plural).
mystery muna.
myth pūrākau.

N

nail nēra.
naked kiri kau, tahanga.
name ingoa.
name, to hua, tapa, whakaingoa.
nap moe.
nappy kope.
narrow whāiti.
nasty kino, maniheko.
nation iwi; motu.
national ā iwi; a te motu, o te motu.
National (political party) Nāhinara.
native māori.
natural tūturu.
nature ao tūroa.
naughty hīanga; nanakia; tutū.
navel pito.
near tata.
nearly tata tonu.
neat tau.
neck kakī, ua.
necklace mau kakī; tāhei.
need hiahia.
needed matea.
needle ngira.
negative (number) tōraro.
neglect whakarere.
neighbour hoatata, kiritata.
nephew irāmutu.
nerve io; uaua.
nervous āmaimai.
nest kōhanga.
net kaharoa; kupenga.
nettle ongaonga.
network hononga; kōtuitui.
neutral kūpapa; whakaraupapa.
never kāhore rawa; kore rawa.

new hou.
New Zealand Aotearoa; Aotearoa me Te Waipounamu; Niu Tīreni.
news kōrero.
newsletter pānui.
newspaper nūpepa.
next (of time) panuku.
nibble kohonihoni, timotimo.
nice rawe; reka; pai.
nickname ingoa kārangaranga, ingoa tāpiri.
niece irāmutu.
night pō.
nightmare kuku, moepapa.
nine iwa.
nip (pinch) kuku, timo.
nipple kōmata; ū.
no kāhore; kānape; kāo (in reply to question); kāore; kore.
no way kore rawa.
noble ariki.
nobody kāore he tangata.
noise turituri, hoihoi, tawetawe.
noisy turituri, hoihoi, tawetawe.
none kāhore.
nonsense kohe, kutukutu ahi.
noon te poupoutanga o te rā.
noose koro.
normal māori; tonu.
north raro; raki.
nose ihu.
nostril pongapanga.
not kāhore, kāore; kore.
notch whakakaniwha.
note (music) orotahi.
note (written) tuhinga.
nothing kore.

notice, a pānui.
notice, to kite.
noticeboard papa pānui.
notion ariā.
November Noema,
Whiringa-ā-rangi.
now āianei, ināianei.
nowhere kāhore he wāhi.
nuclear karihi.
nuclear-free karihi-kau.

nudge tuketuke.
nuisance hōhā; pōrearea.
numb kōpā
number nama.
numberplate tauwaka.
nurse kaihiki (of a child); nāhi,
nēhi.
nurse, to tapuhi.
nut nati.

O

o'clock karaka.
oak, New Zealand pūriri.
oar hoe.
obedient rongo.
obey rongo.
object, to whakakāhore.
obsidian tūhua.
obstacle ārai.
obstinate pake.
obstruct pā.
obtained riro.
occupied kapi.
ocean moana; tai.
ochre, red kōkōwai.
October Oketopa,
    Whiringa-ā-nuku.
octopus wheke.
odd (occasional) tīpakopako;
    (number) panatahi; (strange)
    rerekē.
of ā, ō.
off (off the field) heke, makere;
    (off the road) raro; (rotten)
    pirau; (the game is off, the
    lights are off) kore.
offend tunuhuruhuru.
offering whakahere.
office (workplace) mahi;
    (department; office, study)
    tari.
officer āpiha.
often auau.
oh no! auē!
oh! ai!
oil hinu.
old (of people) kaumātua;
    (of things) tawhito.
omen aituā.
on i, kei, ki; runga.

once kotahi.
one kotahi, tahi.
onion aniana, riki.
only anahe, anake; kau; noa
    iho.
open (adjective) are, puare;
    hāmama; tuwhera; wātea.
open, to huaki; whakatuwhera.
opening puta.
operate (perform surgery)
    tapahi; (use) whakamahi.
operation mahi; (mathematics)
    paheko; (medical) pokanga.
opinion whakaaro.
opportunity wā.
opposite taurite.
oppress pēhi, where.
optician kaimātai whatu.
or rānei.
orange (colour) karaka; (fruit)
    ārani.
orange juice wai ārani.
orator pūkōrero.
orchard uru huarākau.
orchestra tira pūoru.
order, to whakahau.
ordinary māori.
origin tīmatanga, tīmatatanga.
original taketake.
orphan pani.
other atu.
ouch! auē!
our ā mātou, ō mātou; ā māua,
    ō māua; tā māua, tō māua; tā
    mātou, tō mātou; ā tātou, ō
    tātou; tā tātou, tō tātou; ā
    tāua, ō tāua; tā tāua, tō tāua.
    (See Māori – English section
    for distinctions in meaning.)

out ki waho.
outer space ātea tūārangi.
outside waho.
oven hāngi; umu.
over ki runga i.
overcome where.
overdose kai inati.
overflow mānu.
overhang tauwhare.
overhanging are.
overhear rongopuku.
overseas rāwāhi, tāwāhi.

overthrow huri.
overturn porohuri.
owe nama.
owl, New Zealand ruru.
own ake, tupu.
oxygen hāora.
oyster tio.
oystercatcher, variable tōrea pango.
oystercatcher, South Island pied tōrea.
ozone layer pekerangi.

139

P

pace whētoko.
Pacific Ocean Te Moananui-a-Kiwa.
package mōkī, mōkihi.
paddle hoe.
paddock pātiki.
page (book) whārangi.
paid ea.
pain mamae.
painful mamae.
paint, a peita.
paint, to peita, tā.
painting, a whakaahua.
pair (people) tokorua; tōpū.
palace whare kairangi.
pale tuatea.
palisade tīwatawata.
palm (of hand) paro.
pancake panekeke.
panic hopohopo, ohooho.
paper pepa, pukapuka.
parachute hekerangi.
parakeet, red-crowned kākāriki; yellow-crowned kākāriki.
parent matua.
park pāka, pārae.
parliament pāremata.
parrot kākā.
parrot, ground kākāpō.
parrot, mountain kea.
parrot's bill kōwhai ngutu-kākā.
parson-bird tūī.
part wāhi.
particle ngota.
partner hoa; hoa rangatira.
party hākari; pō whakangahau, whakangahau; (political) rōpū.

pass (exam, test) pāhi, puta; (give, hand on) hoatu, homai; (mountain) āpiti, kapiti; (sport, by hand) maka, panga, whiu; (sport, with foot, stick, e.g. hockey, soccer) tuku; (ticket) tīkiti.
pass away hemo, mate.
pass by hipa, pahemo, pahure, taha.
pass down tuku iho.
pass in or out tomo.
pass off whakatū.
pass out hauaitu, tīrehe, tāporepore.
pass over hapa.
pass round (go around) taka; (hand out, distribute) whakarato.
pass through puta.
pass time pau, whakapau.
pass up whakakore.
passage ara.
passenger pāhihi.
passport uruwhenua.
past, the mua.
pasta parāoa rimurapa.
pastime runaruna.
pastry pōhā.
path ara.
patient manawanui; (sick person) tūroro.
pattern tauira.
pause okioki.
pay utu.
pea pī.
peace rangimārie; rongo.
peaceful hūmārie, hūmārire.
peach pītiti.

peak keo, tihi.
peanut pīnati.
peanut butter pīnati pata.
pear pea.
pearl peara.
pebble kōhatu, kōwhatu,
   pōhatu.
pedestrian crossing rewarangi.
peel, to hore, tīhore.
peeled mahihore.
peg titi.
pen pene.
pencil pene rākau.
penguin, blue kororā.
penguin, crested tawaki.
penguin, yellow-eyed hoiho.
penis ure.
penny pene; kapa.
people hunga; iwi; tāngata.
pepper pepa.
pepper-tree horopito.
perch taunga.
perfect tika.
perfume kakara, rautangi.
perhaps pea.
period rangi, takiwā, tau, wā;
   (school) wāhanga;
   (menstruation) mate wahine.
perish mate.
permanent tūturu.
permission whakaaetanga.
permit tuku.
perplexed pōhēhē.
persist ngana.
person kōiwi; tangata.
perspiration kakawa,
   werawera.
persuade kukume.
pest nanakia.
pet mōkai.
petrel, black taikō.
petrel, common diving kuaka.
petrel, Cook's tītī.

petrel, grey-faced ōi.
petrel, mottled kōrure.
petrol hinu.
petrol station teihana hinu.
phone waea.
photocopier pūrere
   whakaahua.
photocopy whakaahua.
photograph whakaahua.
photographer kaiwhakaahua.
piano piana.
pick, a pika.
pick, to kōwhiri, whiriwhiri;
   tīpako.
picnic pikiniki.
picture whakaahua.
pie pae.
piece wāhi.
pierce poka.
pig poaka.
pigeon, New Zealand kererū,
   kūkū, kūkupa.
pigeonwood porokaiwhiria.
pilchard mohimohi.
pile pūranga.
pill pere.
pillow pera; urunga.
pilot kaiurungi.
pimple kiritona.
pin pine, titi.
pinch kini, kuti, nati.
pine, black mataī.
pine, celery tānekaha.
pine, mountain celery toatoa.
pine, radiata paina.
pine, red rimu.
pine, white kahikatea.
pink mākurakura, māwhero.
pipe paipa.
pipit, New Zealand pīhoihoi.
pirate kaitiora.
pistol ngutu pārera.
pit kōrua, rua.

pity aroha; atawhai.
pizza parehe.
place wāhi.
place, to panga.
plain (bare) more; (clear) mārama; (flat land) mānia; (ordinary) māori.
plait raranga, whiri.
plan (course of action) kaupapa; (diagram) hoahoa, tauira.
plane (aeroplane) wakarererangi; (mathematics) papa.
plant, a tipu, tupu.
plant, to tanu; whakatipu; whakatō.
plastic kirihou.
plate pereti.
play tākaro.
playful pukutākaro.
playground papatākaro.
pleasant āhuareka.
please (polite request) koa.
please, to whakawaireka.
pleased koa, uruhau, waingohia.
pleasure rēhia.
plentiful maha, nui, rahi, rere, tini.
plenty huhua.
plough parau.
plover, sand tuturuatu.
plover, New Zealand shore kohutapu.
pluck whawhaki.
plug puru.
plum paramu.
plump kukune, kunekune.
plunder muru.
PO Box pouaka poutāpeta.
pocket pūkoro, pūtea.
pocket money utu ā wiki.

poem pātere; whiti.
point, a mata, tara, tongi.
point, to tohutohu.
poison paitini.
poker kapekape.
polar bear pea hurumā.
pole pou.
police officer pirihimana.
policy kaupapa here.
polite huatau.
politics tōrangapū.
pollen para.
pollute poke.
pollution pokenga.
pond hōpua.
ponder whakaaroaro.
pony poniponi.
pool (of water, blood) hōpua; (swimming) paoro.
poor pōhara, rawakore.
popcorn kānga papā.
porch mahau, roro.
pork poaka.
porous koropungapunga.
position takotoranga; tūnga, tūranga.
possessions rawa, taonga, taputapu.
possible āhei, taea.
post (mail, noun) mēra; (pole) pou; (mail, send) tuku.
post office poutāpeta.
postcard kāri.
postie kaiamo mēra.
pot kōhua.
potato parareka; rīwai; taewa.
pottery kerepeti, matapaia.
pound, a pāuna.
pound, to āki, pao, patu, tuki.
pour ringi, rutu.
pout tupere.
powder paura.
power ihi; mana.

practice (training) whakawaiwai; (application, use) mahi; (custom) hanga, ritenga, tikanga.
practise parakitihi, whakawai.
praise, to mihi; whakamihi; whakanui; whakapai.
pram waka pēpi.
pray īnoi.
prayer karakia.
preach kauwhau.
pregnant hapū.
prepare taka, takatū, whakapai, whakarite, whakatika.
present (gift) koha, whakahere.
present, to tāpae.
preserve rāhui; tiaki.
press down tāmi.
prestige mana.
presume whakahira (be presumptuous).
pretend māminga, takune.
pretty ātaahua.
prevent taupā.
price utu.
prick oka.
pride whakapehapeha.
priest pirihi, piriti; tohunga.
prime minister pirimia.
prince piriniha.
princess piriniha.
principal tumuaki.
principle kaupapa; mātāpono; mauri.
print tā.
print-out pepa.
prion, Antarctic totorore, whirioa.
prion, broad-billed pararā.
prion, fairy tītī wainui.
prison whare herehere.
prisoner mau herehere, pononga.

private tūmataiti.
prize paraihe.
problem mate; raruraru.
profit hua.
project kaupapa.
promise kupu whakaari.
proper tika.
property rawa; taonga.
prophet poropiti.
protect tiaki; whakamarumaru.
protection whakamarumaru.
protest mautohe, tautohe.
protestor waha mautohe.
protrude whererei.
proud whakahīhī.
prove whakamātau.
provoke pātari, whakapātaritari.
psalm waiata.
pub pāparakāuta.
public (adjective) tūmatanui.
public, the iwi whānui.
publish tā, whakaputa.
puddle tōhihi.
pull kume, tō.
pull apart heu.
pull up huti.
pumice koropungapunga.
pumpkin paukena.
punch, to meke.
punish whiu.
punished ngawhi.
pupil (of eye) karupango, kau, whatu, whatupango; (learner) ākonga.
puppet karetao.
purple poroporo.
purpose kaupapa; rawa; tikanga; whakaaro.
purse pāhi.
push pana, tute.
push down tūraki.
push for (advocate) kōkiri.
pushchair waka pēpi.

put whao.
put in komo.
put on (clothes etc) kahu,
  kākahu, kuhu.

put out (extinguish) tinei.
pyjamas kahu moe.

Q

quail, New Zealand koreke (extinct).

quantity nui.

quarantine taratahi.

quarrel wau.

quarter hauwhā, koata.

quartz kiripaka.

queen kuini.

question pātai, ui.

questionnaire rārangi pātai.

queue rārangi.

quick kakama, hihiko, hohoro, tere.

quickly wawe.

quiet wahangū.

quit whakamutu.

quite (adverb) āhua; (certainly) mārika.

quiz kai roro.

quota motunga.

quotation pepeha, kōrero

quote whakahua; (estimate) whakatau utu.

R

rabbit rāpeti.
race (athletics) tauomaoma;
  (contest) whakataetae;
  (people) iwi, uri.
racquet patu.
radar hihiani.
radio reo irirangi.
radioactive ira rukeruke.
raffle rāwhara.
raft, light mōkihi.
rafter heke.
rage niwha, pukuriri.
ragged kuha.
rags karukaru.
rail rēri, rēra.
rail, banded moho-pererū.
rail, Chatham Island
  matirakāhu (extinct).
rail, Dieffenbach's
  moeriki (extinct).
railway rerewhenua.
railway station teihana.
rain ua.
rainbird (mottled petrel)
  korari.
rainbow āniwaniwa, uenuku.
raincoat tāpōrena, uarua.
raise hāpai.
raised tārewa.
raisin karēpe tauraki.
rake rakuraku.
range of hills paeroa.
rank tira.
ransom utu.
rap, to kuru.
rascal nauhea.
rat kiore.
rate (charge) utu; (frequency)
  auau; (speed) pāpātanga.

rather engari.
rattle tetetete.
raw mata.
ray of sun hihi.
razor heu.
reach (arrive, attain) eke, tae;
  (stretch) whakatoro.
read pānui
read aloud pānui.
ready reri; rite; tatanga.
real tinana; tino.
reap katokato.
rear muri.
reason take.
rebel, a tutū.
rebel, to whana.
receive tango.
receptacle takotoranga.
reception (wedding) hākari;
  (radio or television) tangi;
  (hotel, office etc) taupaepae,
  wāhi whakatau.
receptionist kiripaepae.
recipe tohutaka.
recite taki, tātaki, takitaki,
  whiti.
reckless pokerenoa.
recognise kite, mātau, mōhio.
record (noun, music) kōpae
  puoro, rekoata.
record (verb, audio) hopu.
red whero.
reduce whakaiti.
reed raupō.
reef ākau, tau.
reel, to ānewa.
referee kaiwawao.
referendum whakataunga ā
  iwi.

reflection whakaata.
refresh whakahauora.
refrigerator whata mātao.
refuge omanga.
refugee rerenga.
refuse (decline) whakakāhore; (rubbish) para, ota.
region pae, rohe, takiwā, whaitua.
regional ā rohe.
regular auau.
reject whakaparahako.
relate (recite) whiti; (to be conceptually connected to) hāngai.
relation eweewe, huānga, whanaunga; (by marriage) kaireperepe; (distant) epeepe.
relationship hononga; whanaungatanga.
relax whakakorokoro; whakatā.
release wete.
relevant hāngai.
reliable (of information) tika; (of person) pono.
relish kīnaki.
reluctant manawapā.
rely whakawhirinaki.
remain noho; toe.
remainder toenga.
remedy rongoa.
remember mahara.
remind whakamahara.
remote control rou mamao.
remove hura; tango.
rent reti.
repair hanga, tapi, whakapai.
repeat tārua, tuarua, whakahokia.
replace whakakapi.
reply whakahoki, whakautu.
report, a pūrongo.
report, to whakatau.

representative māngai.
reptile ngārara.
request tono.
rescue, a whakaoranga.
rescue, to whakaora.
resist whawhai.
respect koha.
response utu.
responsibility kawenga.
rest (break) whakangā, whakatā; (pause) okioki; (remainder) toenga; (sit on) tau.
restaurant wharekai.
restless tourepa.
result hua; tukunga iho.
return hoki.
revenge ngaki, utu.
reward utu.
rhyme huarite.
ribbon rīpene.
ribbonwood, mountain houhere.
ribs kaokao.
rice raihi.
rich (of food) mōmona; (wealthy) whai rawa, whai taonga.
riddle panga.
ride eke, haere.
ridge hiwi.
ridge-pole tāhū, tāhuhu.
rifleman (bird) tītitipounamu.
right (correct) tika; (direction) katau, matau.
rim niao.
ring (circle) mōwhiti, porohita, porowhita; (jewellery) rīngi, tarawhiti.
ring, to rīngi; waea.
ripe maoa.
ripple kare.
rise ara.

rise up maranga.
river awa.
riverbank parenga.
road ara, huarahi, rori.
roadworks whakatikatikanga
  rori.
roam tipiwhenua.
roar haruru.
roast tunu.
rob tāhae.
robber tāhae.
robin, New Zealand pītoitoi;
  toutouwai.
robot karetao.
rock climbing piki toka.
rock, a kāmaka, toka.
rock, to whakapīoioi.
roll (list of names) rārangi
  ingoa.
roll up pōkai.
roll, to taka.
rollerblades koneke.
rollerskates kopareti.
rollerskating koneke.
roof tuanui.
room rūma.

rooster tame heihei.
root pakiaka; pū.
rootlet weu.
rope taura.
rose, a rōhi.
rotten pirau.
rough pūhungahunga; tara,
  tuatete; tūhourangi.
round taka.
row (line) rārangi, tūtira.
row, to hoe.
royal ariki tapairu.
rub miri, mirimiri.
rubber (eraser) muku.
rubbish otaota.
rudder urungi.
rugby whutupaoro.
ruler (stationery) tauine.
rumble ngunguru, puoro.
run oma.
run away tahuti.
runner kaioma.
runway papa taunga.
rush (plant) kuta; wīwī.
rush, to hīrere, whana.
rust waikura.

S

sack pēke.
sacred tapu.
sad hinapōuri, pōuri.
saddle tera.
saddleback tieke.
sadness hinapōuri, matapōrehu,
  pōuri.
safe ora.
safety whakarurutanga.
sago hēko.
sail, a rā.
sail, to rere, tere.
sailor hēramana.
salad huamata.
salary utu ā tau.
sale hokohoko.
saliva hūware.
salmon hāmana.
salt tote.
salty mātaitai.
salute hongi.
same ōrite, rite.
sand one.
sandal kopa, korehe.
sandbank tāhuna.
sandfly namu.
sandwich hanawiti.
sanitary pad kope.
Santa Claus Hana Kōkō.
sapling kohuri.
satellite amiorangi.
satisfactory pai.
satisfied mākona, manawareka,
  mauru.
Saturday Hātarei, Rāhoroi.
sauce kīnaki; wairanu.
saucepan hōpane.
sausage tōtiti.
save (put away money) tiaki,

tohu, whakaputu;
  (rescue) whakaora.
savings pūtea.
savoury kakara.
saw (wood) kani.
saxophone pūtohe.
say kī; kōrero.
scales (for weighing) whārite.
scandal pakiwaitara.
scar nawe.
scarce papāroa.
scare, a mataku, tumeke.
scare, to whakamataku.
scatter hora.
scattered marara, paratī.
scaup, New Zealand papango.
scent kakara, tīare, tīere.
school kura.
schoolbag pāhi, pēke, kopa.
science pūtaiao.
scientist kaipūtaiao.
scissors kutikuti.
scold whawharo.
scoop out tīkaro, tikarohi.
scorched hunu.
score, the tapeke.
score, to paneke.
scoria rangitoto.
scoundrel taurekareka.
scout tūtai.
scrap toenga.
scrape tahitahi, waru.
scratch, to natu, raku, rapi.
scream hāparangi, ngoengoe.
screech kae.
screen ārai; (computer) mata.
scrub, to kōmukumuku.
sea moana.
seafood kaimoana.

seagull karoro.
seal (marine mammal) kekeno.
search party ohu-rapa.
search, a rapunga.
search, to kimi, rapu.
seashell anga.
seasick ruaki moana.
seaside tātahi.
season tau, wāhanga.
seat, a nohoanga, tūru.
seat, to whakanoho.
seatbelt tātua tūru, whakatina.
seaweed rimurimu.
second (ordinal number)
    tuarua; (unit of time)
    kimonga.
secret muna, tōngā.
secretary hēkeretari.
secure, to runa.
sediment para.
see kite.
seed kākano, kano, purapura.
seek kimi.
seem ngia.
seesaw pīoioi.
select tīpako, whiriwhiri.
self ake; anō; kōiwi.
selfish kanepō, matapiko.
sell hoko.
send ngare; tono; tuku.
send away tono.
sense, to rongo.
sensible (of idea etc) whai
    tikanga.
sentence (grammar) rerenga;
    (prison) whiu.
sentry tūtai.
separate motuhake; tauwehe.
September Hepetema, Mahuru.
series raupapa.
servant kaimahi, pononga.
serve whakarato.
set aside tāpui.

set in order whakapai.
set in place whakatakoto.
set off (on journey) whakatika
    atu.
set on fire tou, tutū.
set up whakatū.
set, a (group) huinga; (tennis)
    tūākari; (theatre) whakarākei.
set, to (congealed) kōpā; (heart,
    mind) whakamau; (sun) tō,
    towene; (to work) tahuri,
    takatū, whakamahi.
seven whitu.
several ētahi, ētehi.
sew tui.
shade maru.
shade, to whakamarumaru.
shadow ātārangi.
shady (of trees) pūruru,
    tāmaru, taumarumaru.
shag, black kawau.
shag, little kawau-paka.
shag, pied kāruhiruhi.
shag, spotted pārekareka.
shake rū, rūrū.
shake gently oioi.
shake hands harirū, rūrū.
shallow koraha, pāpaku.
shame whakamā.
shampoo hopi makawe.
shape ata.
shape, to tārai.
share out tohatoha.
share, a hea, tiri, wakawaka.
shark mako, mangō.
sharp koi.
sharpen whakakoi.
shave heu, waru.
she ia.
shearwater, flesh-footed
    taonui.
shearwater, fluttering
    pakahā.

shearwater, sooty ōi; tītī.
shed wharau.
sheep hipi.
sheet hīti.
shelf pae.
shell anga, pāpapa.
shellfish kaeo.
shelter (protection) maru.
shelter, to whakamarumaru.
shepherd hēpara.
shine korapu.
shingle toetoe.
shiny pīataata.
ship kaipuke; waka.
shipwreck paenga.
shirt hāte.
shiver wiri.
shoal of fish rara.
shock whiti.
shoe hū.
shoelace kaui.
shoot, a ngao, pihi, toro.
shoot, to pupuhi.
shop (store) toa, whare hoko.
shop, to hoko.
shore ākau.
shore plover tuturuatu.
short poto.
short cut poka tata.
shortly potopoto, taro.
shorts tarau poto.
should me.
should not kaua.
shoulder pakihiwi, pokohiwi.
shout hāmama, umere.
shout at hāhā.
shovel koko.
shoveler, Australasian
    kuruwhengi.
show, a konohete,
    whakangahau.
show, to whakaatu.
shower (bathroom) hīrere;

(throw in great numbers)
ringi; (rain) uwhiuwhi.
shriek tarakeha (of birds); tīoro
    (of people).
shrimp potipoti.
shudder oi.
shut kati.
shut (eyes) nenewha; (hand or
    mouth) kuti.
shy whakamā.
sick maki, mate, māuiui.
side taha.
sift tātari.
sigh mapu.
sight (experience, view)
    tirohanga; (vision) kite.
sight, to kite.
sightseeing hōpara.
sign tohu.
silence mūmū.
silent, to be nohopuku, ngū,
    taipā, wahangū.
silly heahea, rorirori.
silver hiriwa.
silvereye tauhou.
similar ōrite.
simple (easy) māmā, ngāwari.
sin hara.
since ina.
sinews uaua.
sing, to waiata.
singer kaiwaiata.
single (unmarried) kiritapu;
    takakau.
sink, to ruku.
sip inuinu.
sister tuahine (of a male);
    tuakana (older of a female);
    taina, teina (younger of a
    female).
sit noho.
six ono.
size nui, rahi.

skateboard papareti.
skeleton anga.
sketch huahua.
ski retihuka.
skiing retireti hukarere.
skin kiri.
skinny tūpuhi.
skipping rope taura piu.
skirt panekoti.
skua, brown hākoakoa.
skull angaanga.
sky rangi.
slam āki.
slant hinga.
slap paki.
slave tūmau.
sledge kōneke, panuku.
sleep moe.
sleeping bag pūngene.
sleepy hiamoe.
sleeve ringaringa.
slice, a poro.
slice, to tapahi.
slide, a retireti.
slide, to koneke, mania, paheke.
slightly tahanga.
slip (landslide) horo.
slip, to mania.
slipper hiripa.
slippery mania.
sloping rōnaki.
slow pōturi, wherū.
slowly āta.
slug ngata.
smack papaki.
small iti, nohinohi (plural
    nonohi), paku, pakupaku, riki
    (plural ririki).
smart (clever) kakama,
    kamakama.
smash āki, tūtuki.
smell (unpleasant) haunga;
    (pleasant) kakara.

smell, to hongi; rongo.
smile memene, menemene,
    mingomingo kata.
smog kōtuhi.
smoke auahi.
smoke, to (cigarettes etc) kai
    paipa; (of fire) paoa.
smooth māeneene.
smother tāmi.
snack paramanawa.
snail ngata.
snake nākahi.
snap (break) whati.
snapper tāmure.
snare rore.
snatch kapo.
sneer tāwai.
sneeze tihe.
sniff hongi.
snore ngongoro.
snorkel ngongohā.
snort whengu.
snow huka.
so (that) kia.
so (therefore) heoi anō, nō
    reira.
soak, to waiwai.
soap hopi.
sob whakaingoingo.
soccer poikiri.
social (adjective) hapori.
social worker tauwhiro.
sock tōkena.
sofa hōpa.
soft ngāwari, ngehengehe,
    ngohengohe.
soft drink waireka.
softly ngāwari.
software pūmanawa rorohiko.
soil oneone.
solar power pūngao kōmaru.
solar system rerenga o
    Tamanuiterā.

soldier hōia.
sole, common pātiki rori.
sole of foot raparapa.
solid pāmārō.
solitary moke.
solution rongoā.
some he; ētahi, ētehi; tētahi, tētehi.
somebody tētahi tangata.
something tētahi mea.
sometimes ētahi wā.
somewhat hanga.
somewhere tētahi wāhi.
son tama.
song waiata.
soon āianei, ākuanei, mea kau ake, nāwai; wawe.
soothe miri.
sore mamae; mate.
sorrowful pōuri; tuarea.
sorry (apology) aroha mai; (sad) pōuri.
sort tū; momo, tūmomo.
sort, to wehewehe.
soul wairua.
sound tangi.
soup hupa.
sour kawa.
source pū, pūkaki; tāuru.
south runga; tonga.
sovereignty rangatiratanga.
sow (seed) rui.
space wā, wāhi, tiriwā; (outer) ātea tūārangi.
spaceship waka tūārangi.
spade kāheru.
spaniard, wild kurikuri.
spark kora.
sparrow tiutiu.
speak kōrero.
speak softly kōhimu, kuihi.
spear huata; tao.
speargrass kurikuri.

special (prized) hirahira; (different) motuhake.
special effects ariā hirahira.
spectacles mōwhiti.
speech (lecture, talk) kauhau, kauwhau, kōrero; (way of talking) reo.
speechless ngū.
speed tere.
speed camera kāmera tere.
speed limit pae tere.
speedboat wakatere.
spell, a karakia.
spell, to tātaki.
spelling tātaki kupu.
spend whakapau.
spider pūngaiwerewere, pūngāwerewere.
spider's web tukutuku.
spike tara.
spill maringi.
spin round takahurihuri.
spinach, New Zealand rengarenga.
spines tuaitara.
spirit wairua.
spit tuha, tuwha.
splash pōrutu.
splinter maramara.
split tītore.
spoil takakino.
spokesperson māngai.
sponge hautai.
spoon koko, pūnu.
spoonbill, royal kōtuku ngutupapa.
sport hākinakina.
sport, to tākaro.
spot tongi.
spotted kōtingotingo.
spouse hoa, hoa rangatira.
sprat kūpae.
spray rehutai.

spread pani.
spread out uhi, uwhi.
spread over popoki.
spring (season) kōanga;
(of water) puna.
spring, to tūrapa.
sprinkle toutou.
sprout pihi.
spy tūtai.
square tapawhā rite.
squeal wē.
squeeze roromi.
squid ngū.
stab pūmuka.
stable (firm, steady, constant)
pūmau, ū, whena; (horse)
tēpara.
stack pū.
stage atamira.
stagger takarangi.
stairs araheke, arawhata.
stalk, a kakau, tā.
stalk, to āngi,
whakamokamoka.
stamp (postage) pane kuini;
(with foot) takahi.
stand firm whakawheua.
stand, to tū.
star whetū.
stare tiro mākutu.
starfish pātangatanga.
start in alarm tumeke, whiti.
start, to tīmata; whakatika.
startle whakaoho.
starve whakatina.
station teihana.
stationary whakapahoho.
stationery pānga tuhituhi.
stay noho.
steady pāmārō.
steak motū.
steal kaiā; tāhae; tipua, tupua;
whānako.

stealthy kōnihi.
steam mamaha, mamaoa.
steep paritū.
steer urungi.
stem tātā.
step whētoko.
stereo tīwharawhara.
stern (noun) kei.
stick, a rākau; tokotoko.
stick, to whakapiri.
sticking plaster tāpi.
sticky hāpiapia, tāpiapia.
stiff kōpā.
still (not moving) marino,
nohopuku; (yet) anō, tonu.
stilt, black kakī.
stilt, pied poaka.
sting kakati.
stingray, short-tailed whai.
stingy matapiko.
stinking piro.
stir kōrori.
stitch tuitui.
stitchbird hihi.
stocking tōkena.
stomach puku.
stone kōhatu, kōwhatu, pōhatu,
pōwhatu.
stool tūru.
stoop tūpou.
stop (command) kāti,
whakamutua.
stop, a tūnga.
stop, to mutu; tū; whakamutu;
whakatū.
store whare hoko.
storehouse pātaka.
storm āwhā, marangai, tūpuhi.
stormy marangai, totoa.
story kōrero; kōrero pūrakau.
stove kare, umu.
straggle tūtārere.
straight tautika, tika, tōtika.

strange tauhou.
stranger tauhou.
strangle tārore.
strap kawe.
straw takakau.
strawberry rōpere.
stream awa, manga.
street tiriti.
strength kaha, whirikoka.
stretch, to totoro, whakatoro.
stride tōihi.
strike (hit) pāike, tākiri;
    (industrial action) auporo.
strike against tūtuki.
strike with fist moto.
string aho.
strip, to tīhore.
stripe tāhei.
striped whakahekeheke.
stroke, to hokomirimiri.
strong kaha.
struck pā, whara.
struggle wheta.
stubborn ioio.
student ākonga, tauira.
study, a tari, whare tuhituhi.
study, to ako.
stumble tapepa.
stump tumutumu.
stupid kūare; moho; pōrangi;
    rorirori; wairangi.
subject, a kaupapa; marau.
submarine waka
    whakatakere.
subsidy pūtea tāpiri.
substitute whakakapi.
subtract tango.
suburb tapa tāone.
such as that pēnā, pērā.
such as this pēnei.
suck momi, ngote.
suddenly tata.
suffer mate.

sugar huka.
suicide, to commit
    whakamomori.
suit (clothing) hūtu.
suitable pai.
sulphur whanariki.
sum tapeke.
summer raumati.
summit taumata; tihi.
sun rā.
sunbathe pāinaina.
sunburn tīkākā.
Sunday Rātapu.
sunglasses mōwhiti rā.
sunny paki.
sunrise whitinga o te rā.
sunscreen pare tīkākā.
sunset tōnga o te rā.
sunshine rāwhiti.
supermarket hokomaha.
supper hapa.
supple ngāwari.
supplejack kareao.
support tautoko; whakaū.
suppose māhara, māharahara.
surf (noun) karekare.
surf, to whakaheke ngaru.
surface mata.
surfboard kōpapa.
surname ingoa whānau.
surprise kōmutu, tumeke.
surprising whakamīharo.
surrender tuku.
surround hautoki.
survey rūri.
surveyor kairūri.
survive ora.
survivor mōrehu, rerenga.
suspicious tūpato.
swallow horomi.
swamp mātā, repo.
swamp hen pūkeko.
swan wani.

sweat tokakawa, werawera.
sweatshirt poraka.
sweep tahi.
sweet reka.
sweetheart tahu, whaiāipo.
swell, to pupuhi.
swift tere.
swim kau; kauhoe; kaukau.

swimming pool hāpua,
  kauranga.
swing tārere.
switch on whakakā.
switch, a pana.
swollen pupuhi, uruumu.
sword hoari.
symbol waitohu.

T

table tēpu.
table tennis poikōpiko.
tablecloth takapapa.
tablespoon kokotaha.
tackle rutu.
tail (of a fish or reptile) hiku;
  (of other animals) waero,
  whiore.
take tango.
take hold of mau, tango.
take off hura, unu.
taken riro.
tale pakiwaitara, pūrākau.
talents parapara.
talk kōrero.
talkative ngutu momoho.
tall roa, tāroaroa; teitei.
tame rata.
tape deck hopureo.
tape, a rīpene.
tape, to hopu.
taper, to hume.
taste hā.
tattered karukaru.
tattoo, a moko.
tattoo, to tā, tā moko.
tax tāke.
taxi wakatono.
tea tī.
teach ako; whakaako.
teacher kaiako, kaiwhakaako,
  māhita.
teal, brown pāteke.
teal, grey tētē.
team kapa, tīma.
teapot tīpāta.
tear off kōwhaki.
tear, to haehae.
tears roimata.

tease whakatoi.
teaspoon kokoiti.
teat ū; kōmata.
tea-tree mānuka.
technology hangarau.
teddy bear teti pea.
teeth niho.
telephone waea.
telephone number nama waea.
television pouaka whakaata.
tell kī, kōrero, whakapuaki,
  whāki.
tell off kōwhete, riri.
temper (anger) riri.
temperature mahana.
temple rae.
temporary rangitahi.
tempt tahu; whakamātautau;
  whakawai.
ten ngahuru; tekau.
tennis tēnehi.
tent tēneti.
term (word) kupu; (period of
  time) wā; (school) wāhanga.
term, to karanga, kī.
tern, black-fronted tara.
tern, Caspian tara-nui.
tern, fairy tara-iti.
tern, white-fronted tara.
terrible wehi.
terror mataku, wehi, wiwini.
terrorist kaiwhakatuma.
test whakamātautau.
testicles raho.
than i.
thank whakamihi,
  whakawhetai.
thank you kia ora, tēnā koe,
  tēnā kōrua, tēnā koutou.

that ia; koinā, koirā; nāna; tēnā (near you); tērā (over there, far away); taua (already mentioned).
the te (singular); ngā (plural).
theatre whare tapere.
theft whānako.
their tā rāua, tō rāua, tā rātou, tō rātou (singular); ā rāua, ō rāua, ā rātou, ō rātou (plural).
them rāua (two); rātau, rātou (more than two).
theme kaupapa.
then kātahi.
theory ariā.
there anā, arā; konā, korā; reira.
therefore nā reira, nō reira.
these ēnei; koinei.
they rāua (two); rātau, rātou (three or more).
thick mātotoru.
thief kaiā, tāhae.
thigh hūhā, kūwhā.
thin kōhoi; maiaka; tūpuhi; whīroki.
thing mea; taru.
think whakaaro.
third tuatoru.
third, a hautoru.
thirst hiainu, hiawai.
thirsty hiainu, hiawai.
this koinei; tēnei.
thistle kōtimana.
thorn tara.
thoroughly mārire.
those (already mentioned) aua; (nearby, near you) ēnā; (over there, far off) ērā.
thought mahara, whakaaro.
thoughtless ware, wareware.
thousand mano.
thread miro.

threat turituri.
threaten wananga.
three toru.
throat kakī, takakī.
throb whetuki.
throne torōna.
through mā; nā.
throughout puta noa.
throw epa, maka, panga, whiu.
throw away ākiri.
thrush, New Zealand piopio (extinct).
thrust kōkiri.
thumb kōnui, rongomatua, tokonui, tōnui.
thump kuru.
thunder whaitiri, whatitiri.
thunderstorm rautupu.
Thursday Rāpare, Tāite.
tick (not cross) tohu.
ticket tīkiti.
tickle whakakoekoe, whakangaoko.
tidal wave tai āniwhaniwha.
tide tai.
tie whītoki.
tie in a knot pona.
tie up here.
tiger taika.
tightly kita.
timber rākau.
time takiwā, wā.
timetable wātaka.
timid taiatea; waitau.
tin tini.
tiny itiiti.
tip hiku.
tiptoe hītekiteki.
tired ngenge, tauwherū.
tissue aikiha pepa.
title ingoa.
to hei; kei; ki.
toad poroka taratara.

toadstool ipurangi.
toast tōhi.
toaster tāina.
tobacco tupeka.
today te rā nei, tēnei rā.
toe korokoro, matimati.
toenail matikuku.
toffee tawhe.
together tahi.
toilet whare iti, wharepaku.
toilet paper pepa whēru,
  whēru.
tolerant ngāwari.
tomato tōmato.
tomorrow ākengokengo,
  aoināke, āpōpō.
tomtit, North Island miromiro.
tomtit, South Island ngirungiru.
ton tana.
tone reo.
tongs pīnohi.
tongue (anatomy) arero;
  (language) reo.
tonight te pō nei, tēnei pō.
tonne tana.
too anō.
tool pāraha, taputapu.
tooth niho.
toothache niho tunga.
toothbrush paraihe niho.
toothpaste paniaku.
top tāuru.
top, whipping kaitaka, pōtaka.
topic kaupapa.
topknot tikitiki.
torch rama.
torn pakaru, tīhaea.
tortoise honu whenua.
toss whiu.
total tapeke.
touch pā.
tough mārō, uaua.
tourist tāpoi.

tow, to taki; tō.
towards kī; mai; (used as a
  prefix only) whaka.
towel tauera.
tower taumaihi.
town tāone.
toy taonga tākaro.
toy with whakapātaritari.
trace (search for) whai; (draw)
  whakaata.
track ara.
track, to taki, whai.
tracksuit kaka rēhia.
tractor tarakihana, tarakitara.
trade (commerce) hokohoko;
  (job) mahi; (swap) tuopu.
train, a rerewhenua, tereina.
train, to (aim) tohu; (teach)
  whakaako, whakangungu;
  (practise) whakawai.
training (skills development)
  whakangungu; (practice,
  session) whakawaiwai.
trample takahi.
trampoline tūraparapa.
translate whakamāori; (into
  English) whakapākehā.
transparent kōataata.
transport waka.
transport, to hari, kawe, mau.
trap māhanga, tarahanga.
travel around hāereere,
  kaihora, pōkai.
travel, to haere; tāwhe.
travellers (group) pahī, ope,
  rei, tere, tira, whananga.
tread takahi.
treasure, a kahurangi; taonga.
treasure, to kaingākau.
treat badly tūkino.
treat well manaaki.
treat, to whakamaimoa.
treatment rongoā.

tree rākau.
tremble wiri, wiriwiri.
trevally araara.
trial whakamātauranga.
tribe iwi; āti, ngāti, ngāi; pū.
trick whakangaio.
trickle totō.
tricycle taraihikara.
trim tahi.
trip, a haerenga.
trip, to hīrawea.
tropic bird, red-tailed
   amokura.
trot toitoi.
trouble raru, raruraru.
trousers tarau.
trout taraute.
truck taraka.
true pono.
trumpet pūtātara.
trunk (tree) tīwai.
trust whakapono;
   whakawhirinaki.

truth pono.
try, to whakamātau.
T-shirt tī hāte.
tube ngongo.
tuberculosis kohitā.
Tuesday Rātū, Tūrei.
tune rangi.
tunnel arapoka.
turn tahuri.
turn on (appliance etc)
   whakakā.
turn to whakaarorangi.
turnip tōnapi.
turnip, wild kōrau.
turtle honu.
twice tuarua.
twilight rikoriko.
twin māhanga.
twinkle hīnātore, kapokapo.
twist whiri.
two rua.
type tū, momo, tūmomo.
typewriter pae patopato.

U

udder ū.
ugly paraheahea.
umbrella marara.
umpire kaiwawao.
uncertain pāhekeheke.
uncle matua, matua kēkē.
uncommon haraki, waraki.
unconscious mauri moe.
undecided whēangaanga.
under ki raro i.
underdone kānewha.
understand mārama; mōhio.
understandable mārama.
underwater whakatakere.
underwear kōpū, tarau.
unemployed kore mahi.
unemployed, the hunga kore
  mahi.
unfinished kohuku.
unfriendly atawhai kino.
ungrateful manawapā.
unhappy pōuri.
unhealthy aewa, āhua mate.
unhurt ora.
uniform kākahu ōrite.
unify whakakotahi.
unimportant iti.
union hononga.
unique ahurei.
universe ao tukupū.
university whare wānanga.
unless ki te kore.
unlucky whakarapa.

unmarried kiritapu; takakau.
unpaid tārewa.
unpleasant houhou.
unpopular kiriweti.
unripe kānewha.
untie takiri, wete.
until ā, āpānoa, tae noa ki.
untrustworthy ngutu tere.
unusual rerekē.
unwelcome waingaio.
unwilling whakatohetohe.
up ki runga.
upset matawai, matawaia.
upside down kōaro.
upstairs pārunga.
upwards ake.
urban tāone.
urge akiaki, tūwhana.
urgent whāwhai.
urinate mimi.
urine mimi.
us māua (us two, but not you);
  tāua (us two, you and me);
  tātou (all of us, everyone);
  mātou (us, but not you).
use (noun) kaha hiahiatanga
  pēnā painga
use, to mau, tango, tangotango,
  whakamahi.
used to (accustomed) waia;
  (past habitual action) tonu.
useful whaihua.
useless koretake.

V

vacant hāmama; kau; wātea.
vacuum cleaner hororē.
vagina tara, teke.
vain whakahīhī,
  whakapehapeha.
valley awaawa, riu, whārua.
valuable tino taonga.
value, to kaingākau.
van kōporo.
vandal kaiauru.
vanish ngaro.
vase ipu.
vegetable huawhenua (fruit or
  product of the ground).
vegetarian kaimanga,
  kaiotaota.
vegetation otaota.
veil ārai.
vein uaua.
velcro piripiri.
vending machine mīhini hoko.
verandah haurangi, mahau,
  roro.
vermin kutu, iroiro.
very rawa, tino.
vessel (container) ipu.
vet, a rata kararehe.
veteran ika a Whiro.

vice kino.
victim (killed in war) ika.
victory wikitōria.
video camera kāmera ataata.
video game tākaro ataata.
video recorder hopu ataata.
videotape rīpene ataata.
view (opinion) titiro; (outlook)
  kainga kanohi, tirohanga.
vigorous tūkaha.
village kāinga; pā.
vine aka.
vineyard māra wāina.
violent whakawiriwiri.
virgin puhi.
virtual reality whaihanga.
virus wheori.
vision kitenga.
visit toro; whakatau.
visitors manuhiri.
vitality hauora.
vitals ngākau.
vocabulary rārangi kupu.
voice reo; waha.
volcano puia.
vomit ruaki.
vote pōti.
voyage rerenga.

W

wade kau.
wag whiuwhiu.
wage utu.
wail whakatautau.
waist hope.
wait tatari.
waiting list rārangi tatari.
wake whakaara.
wakeful whakawhetū.
walk haere mā raro, hīkoi.
wall (freestanding) taiepa; (of house, building) pakitara.
wallet kopa.
wand tira.
wander ānau.
wanderer taurangi.
want, to hiahia, pīrangi.
war pakanga.
warbler, grey riroriro.
wardrobe kāpata kākahu.
warm mahana.
warm, to whakamahana.
warn whakatūpato.
warrior toa.
wary matakana.
wash horoi.
washing machine pūrere horoi.
wasp katipō.
waste (of time, effort etc) maumau, moumou.
wasteful ngutu hore.
watch, a wati.
watch, to mātai, mātaki, mātakitaki.
watchful mataara, tūmatohi.
water wai; (fresh) waimāori; (salt) waitai.
waterfall hīrere, rere.
watering can kēna wai.

waterproof pihi, piri.
water-skiing retiwai.
wave (arm) pōhiri, pōwhiri, tīwhaiwhai; (surf) ngaru.
waxeye tauhou.
way āhua, āhuatanga; ara, huarahi; tikanga.
we (one other person and I) māua; (we, you and I) tāua; (we all) tātou; (we but not you) mātou.
weak ānewa, ngoikore, pōrorotua.
weaken wheroku.
weakness wairuhi.
wealth rawa, taonga.
wealthy whai rawa, whai taonga.
weapon patu.
wear mau.
wear out taiākotikoti.
weary ngenge.
weather āhua o te rangi, huarere, rangi.
weave raranga.
web tukutuku.
wedding mārenatanga.
wedge matakahi, ora.
Wednesday Rāapa, Wenerei.
weed, to ngaki.
weeds otaota.
week rāwhitu, wiki.
weekend mutunga wiki, paunga rāwhitu.
weep tangi.
weigh ine taumaha.
weight taumaha.
weir pā.
welcome haere mai; kia ora.

welcome karanga; pōwhiri.
well (healthy) ora.
well! ehi!
Wellington Te Whanganui-a-Tara.
west hauāuru, taitua, uru.
Western Pākehā.
wet mākū.
whale parāoa; tohorā.
wharf wāpu.
what aha.
what! are!
what? he aha?
wheat witi.
wheel porowhita, wīra.
wheelbarrow huripara.
wheelchair kōrea.
wheezing tīmohu.
when ana, ina; ka; ua.
when? (used of the future) āhea?, āwhea?; (used of the past) inahea?, inawhea?, nōnahea?, nōnawhea?
whence? nōhea?
whenever (everytime) kia; (sometime) mā te wā.
where from? i hea?, i whea?; (originally) nō hea?, nō whea?
where? hea; kei hea?, kei whea?
whether ahakoa.
which mea.
which? (singular) tēhea?, tēwhea?; (plural) ēhea?, ēwhea?.
while ahakoa; i, kai, kei, keiwhā, koi; wā.
whip wepu.
whip, to whiu.
whirlpool āwhiowhio.
whirlwind āwhiowhio.
whisper kōhimu, whetewhete.
whistle whio.

white mā, tea.
whitebait īnanga.
whiteboard papa tuhituhi.
whitehead pōpokotea; tateko.
who mea; (future) mā; (past) nā; nāna.
who? ko wai?; wai?
whole katoa.
whose? nā wai?; nō wai?
why? he aha ai?; mō te aha?
wicked kino.
wide whānui.
widow pani, pouaru.
widower pouaru.
width whānui.
wife hoa wahine, wahine.
wiggle hīkaikai.
wild māka.
wild irishman tūmatakuru.
wildlife ngā tini a Tāne.
will wira.
willing pai.
win toa.
wind hau.
winding kōpiko.
windmill hurihau.
window mataaho, matapihi.
windscreen mataaho waka.
windsurfing mirihau.
windy hauhau.
wine wāina.
wineberry makomako.
wing parirau.
wink kimo.
winkle pūpū.
winner toa.
winter hōtoke, makariri, takurua.
wipe miri; ūkui; (bottom) whēru.
wire waea.
wisdom mōhiotanga.
wise pūkenga.

wish hiahia, pīrangi.
witch wahine mākutu.
with i; kei; ki; me; hei.
withered rio.
wizard ruānuku.
wolf wūruhi.
woman wahine.
womb kōpū.
women wāhine.
wonder (suppose) māharahara.
wonder at mīharo.
wonderful whakamīharo.
wood rākau.
wooden rākau.
woodhen weka.
wool wūru.
woollen wūru.
word kupu.
word processor punenga kupu.
work mahi.
worker kaimahi.
world ao.
worm noke, toke.
worn out waitau.

worry āwangawanga, māharahara.
worse kino ake.
worship karakia.
worthless koretake.
worthwhile whaihua.
worthy pai.
wound tūnga.
wrap kōpaki.
wreath pare.
wreck, a paenga.
wreck, to tukituki.
wren, bush mātuhi (extinct).
wrestle tākaro.
wriggle kori, korikori.
wring whakawiri.
wrinkle rehe.
wrinkled kūwhewhewhewhe.
wrist kawititanga o te ringaringa.
write tuhituhi.
writhe tāwheta.
wrong hē.

X Y Z

x-ray hihi kōkiri
xylophone pakakau.
yacht pere rua.
yam oka; uhi, uwhi.
yard iāri.
yawn hāmamamama, hītako, kōwaha, kowhera, tūwaharoa.
year tau.
yearn kōingo, kōnohi.
yell horu.
yellow kōwhai, pungapunga.
yellow-eyed penguin hoiho.
yellowhead mohua.
yes āe.
yesterday inanahi.
yet anō.
yield tuku.
yoghurt waipupuru.
yolk tōhua.
yonder rā.
you (singular) koe; (you two) kōrua; (you, three or more) koutou.
young (of people) taitamariki, tamariki; (of animals) kūao, punua.

young person rangatahi, taiohi, taitamariki.
your (one person, singular) tāu, tō, tōu; (two people, singular) tā kōrua, tō kōrua; (three or more people, singular) ta koutou, tō koutou; (one person, plural) āu, ō, ōu; (two people, plural) ā kōrua, ō kōrua; (three or more people, plural) ā koutou, ō koutou.
yours nāu, nōu.
youth (young person) rangatahi, taiohi, taitamariki; (period of life) oinga, taiohinga, taitamarikitanga, whanaketanga.
zebra hepapa.
zebra crossing rewarangi.
zero kore.
zip kōtui.
zone rohe.
zoo papa kararehe.

Vocabulary Lists

Ngā Mihi me ngā Poroporoaki
Greetings and Farewells

e noho rā	farewell (said by those leaving).
haere rā	farewell (said by those remaining behind).
hei konā	goodbye (on telephone)
hei konei rā	farewell (said by those leaving).
kia ora	hello, welcome.
tēnā koe	hello (to one person).
tēnā kōrua	hello (to two people).
tēnā koutou	hello (to three or more people).

Ngā Wāhanga o te Tau
Seasons

hōtoke, takurua, makariri	winter.
kōanga, mahuru	spring.
raumati	summer.
ngahuru	autumn.

Ngā Rā o te Wiki
Days of the Week

Rāhina	Mane	Monday.
Rātū	Tūrei	Tuesday.
Rāapa	Wenerei	Wednesday.
Rāpare	Tāite	Thursday.
Rāmere	Paraire	Friday.
Rāhoroi	Hātarei	Saturday.
Rātapu	Rātapu	Sunday.

Ngā Marama o te Tau
Months of the Year

Kohitātea	Hānuere	January.
Huitanguru	Pēpuere	February.
Poutūterangi	Māehe	March.
Paengawhāwhā	Āperira	April.
Haratua	Mei	May.
Pipiri	Hune	June.
Hōngongoi	Hūrae	July.
Hereturikōkā	Ākuhata	August.
Mahuru	Hepetema	September.
Whiringa-ā-nuku	Oketopa	October.
Whiringa-ā-rangi	Noema	November.
Hakihea	Tīhema	December.

Ngā Tae
Colours

black	mangu, pango.
blue	kahurangi, kikorangi, purū.
brown	pōuriuri, parauri, paraone.
gold	kōura.
green	kākāriki.
grey	tārekoreko.
orange	karaka.
pink	mākurakura, māwhero.
purple	poroporo.
red	whero.
silver	hiriwa.
white	mā, tea.
yellow	kōwhai, pungapunga.

Ngā Nama
Numbers

tahi	one.
rua	two.
toru	three.
whā	four.
rima	five.
ono	six.

whitu	seven.
waru	eight.
iwa	nine.
tekau; ngahuru	ten.
tekau mā tahi	eleven.
tekau mā rua	twelve.
tekau mā toru	thirteen.
rua tekau	twenty.
kotahi rau	one hundred.
e rima rau	five hundred.
kotahi mano	one thousand.
e rima mano	five thousand.
kotahi miriona	one million.
kotahi piriona	one billion.

- Numbers one to nine are preceded by 'e' whether they are indicating ones, hundreds or thousands, e.g. e rima = five, e toru rau = three hundred.
- Kotahi is used for the 1 in 100, 1,000 etc.
- Numbers 11 to 19 are formed by adding the number 10, e.g. tekau mā rima = 15.
- Numbers 20 to 90 are formed by placing the number in front of 10, e.g. iwa tekau = 90.
- A specimen number will indicate the system, e.g. e iwa mano kotahi rau e waru tekau mā rua = 9,182.
- When counting aloud prefix numbers one to nine with 'ka', e.g. ka tahi, ka rua, ka toru = one, two, three.

Ngā Ingoa
Māori names

Ānaru	Andrew.
Ani	Ann.
Ārana	Alan.
Arapeta	Albert.
Arapeti	Alfred.
Arekahānara	Alexander.
Arihia	Alice.
Atonio	Anthony.
Ēmere	Emily.
Erihāpeti	Elizabeth.

Eruera	Edward.
Erueti	Edward.
Hare	Charles.
Hēmi	James, Jimmy.
Hēnare	Henry.
Hēni	Jane, Jenny.
Hoani	John.
Hōhepa	Joseph.
Hōne	John.
Hōri	George.
Kahi	Guy; Gus.
Kātarina	Catherine.
Māka	Mark.
Mākareta	Margaret.
Māta	Martha.
Matiu	Matthew.
Mere	Mary.
Mikaere	Michael.
Paora	Paul.
Pererika	Frederick.
Piripi	Philip.
Pita	Peter.
Rāhera	Rachel.
Rāwiri	David.
Rewi	Louis.
Ruihi	Lucy.
Tāmati	Thomas.
Tārati	Dorothy.
Tīpene	Stephen.
Tiaki	Jack; Jackie.
Tiare	Charlie.
Wāta	Walter.
Wiremu	William.

Ngā Taone Nunui o Aotearoa
New Zealand Cities

Auckland	Tāmaki-makau-rau.
Christchurch	Ōtautahi.
Dunedin	Ōtepoti.
Gisborne	Tūranganui-a-Kiwa.
Hamilton	Kirikiriroa.

Hastings	Heretaunga.
Invercargill	Murihiku.
Napier	Ahuriri.
Nelson	Whakatū.
New Plymouth	Ngamotu.
Palmerston North	Papaioea.
Wellington	Pōneke; Whanga-nui-a-Tara.

Ngā Manu
Birds

akiaki	red-billed gull.
amokura	red-tailed tropic bird.
hākoakoa	brown skua (sea hawk).
hihi	stitchbird.
hoiho	yellow-eyed penguin.
huia	huia (extinct).
kāhu	Australasian harrier (hawk).
kākā	native parrot or kākā.
kākāpō	ground parrot or kākāpō.
kākāriki	red-crowned parakeet; yellow-crowned parakeet.
kakī	black stilt.
karakahia	grey duck.
kārearea	New Zealand falcon (bush hawk).
karoro	black-backed gull.
kāruhiruhi	pied shag.
kawau	black shag.
kawau-paka	little shag.
kea	kea (mountain parrot).
kererū	wood pigeon.
kiwi	kiwi (brown kiwi).
kiwi-pukupuku	little spotted kiwi.
kohutapu	New Zealand shore plover.
kōkako	blue-wattled crow; orange-wattled crow.
kōkō	tūī.
kōpara	bellbird.
korari	mottled petrel, rainbird.
korimako	bellbird.
kororā	blue penguin.
kōtare	kingfisher.
kōtuku	white heron.

kōtuku-ngutupapa	royal spoonbill.
kūaka	common diving petrel; eastern bar-tailed godwit.
kūkū	New Zealand pigeon.
kuruwhengi	Australasian shoveler.
makomako	bellbird.
mātātā	fernbird.
matuku-hurepō	Australasian bittern.
matuku-moana	white-faced heron; reef heron.
miromiro	North Island tomtit.
moa	moa (extinct).
moho-pererū	banded rail.
mōhua	yellowhead.
ngirungiru	South Island tomtit.
ōi	sooty shearwater (muttonbird); grey-faced petrel.
pakahā	fluttering shearwater.
pāpango	New Zealand scaup (black teal).
pararā	broad-billed prion.
pārekareka	spotted shag.
pārera	grey duck.
pāteke	brown teal.
pīhoihoi	New Zealand pipit.
pīpipi	brown creeper.
pīpīwharauroa	shining cuckoo.
pītoitoi	New Zealand robin.
pīwakawaka	fantail (North Island fantail; South Island fantail).
poaka	pied stilt.
pōpokotea	whitehead.
pūkeko	swamp hen.
pūtangitangi	paradise duck.
pūteketeke	crested grebe.
pūweto	spotless crake.
riroriro	grey warbler.
roa	great spotted kiwi.
rupe	pigeon.
ruru	morepork (New Zealand owl).
tāiko	black petrel.
takahē	takahē (South Island takahē).
tākapu	Australasian gannet.
tākupu	Australasian gannet.
taonui	flesh-footed shearwater.

tara	black-fronted tern; white-fronted tern.
tara-iti	fairy tern.
tara-nui	Caspian tern.
tarāpunga	black-billed gull; red-billed gull.
tātāeko	whitehead.
tauhou	silvereye.
tawaki	Fiordland crested penguin; Snares crested penguin.
tētē	grey teal.
tīeke	saddleback.
tīrairaka	fantail (North Island fantail; South Island fantail).
tītī	sooty shearwater or muttonbird; Cook's petrel.
tītī wainui	fairy prion.
tītitipounamu	rifleman.
tīwaiwaka	(North Island fantail; South Island fantail).
tīwakawaka	(North Island fantail; South Island fantail).
tōrea	South Island pied oystercatcher.
tōrea-pango	variable oystercatcher.
toroa	wandering albatross; black-browed mollymawk.
toroa-haunui	light-mantled sooty albatross.
toroa-whakaingo	southern royal albatross; northern royal albatross.
totoeka	brown kiwi.
totorore	Antarctic prion.
toutouwai	New Zealand robin.
tūī	tūī or parson bird.
tuturiwhatu	New Zealand dotterel.
tuturuatu	shore plover.
weka	woodhen; buff woodhen.
weweia	New Zealand dabchick.
whio	blue duck.

Ngā Rākau

Trees

akatea	white-flowered rātā vine.
akeake	akeake.
hīnau	hīnau.
horoeka	lancewood.
horopito	pepper-tree.

houhere	ribbonwood; lacebark (hoheria).
kahikatea	kahikatea (white pine).
kaikōmako	kaikōmako.
kāmahi	kāmahi.
kānuka	kanuka.
karaka	karaka (New Zealand laurel).
kauri	kauri.
kāwaka	New Zealand arbor vitae.
kawakawa	kawakawa (pepper-tree).
kohekohe	kohekohe (New Zealand cedar).
kōhūhū	kōhūhū.
kōhutuhutu	tree fuchsia.
kōtukutuku	kōtukutuku (tree fuchsia).
kōwhai	kōwhai.
kōwhai ngutu-kākā	kākā's beak (red kōwhai, parrot's bill).
māhoe	māhoe.
maire	maire.
maire-tawake	marie-tawake (black maire).
makamaka	makamaka.
makomako	makomako (wineberry).
manawa	mangrove.
mānuka	mānuka (tea-tree)
māpau	māpau.
mataī	mataī (black pine).
miro	miro.
nīkau	nīkau.
ngaio	ngaio.
poataniwha	poataniwha.
pōhutukawa	pōhutukawa (New Zealand Christmas tree).
porokaiwhiria	pigeon wood.
puka	puka (broadleaf).
pukatea	pukatea.
punawētā	Māori may.
pūriri	pūriri or New Zealand oak.
putaputawētā	Māori may.
ramarama	ramarama.
rātā	rātā.
raukawa	raukawa.
rewarewa	Māori honeysuckle (New Zealand honeysuckle).
rimu	rimu (red pine).
rōhutu	rōhutu.
tānekaha	tānekaha (celery pine).

taraire	taraire.
tarata	tarata (lemonwood).
tawa	tawa.
tāwari	tāwari.
tāwheowheo	tāwheowheo (New Zealand lilac).
tāwhero	tāwhero.
tawhiwhi	tawhiwhi.
tī-kouka	cabbage tree.
tītoki	tītoki (New Zealand ash).
toatoa	mountain toatoa.
toro	toro.
tōtara	tōtara.
tutu	tutu ('toot').
wharangi	wharangi.
whau	whau.
whauwhau	five-finger.

Ngā Tini a Tangaroa
Sea Creatures

araara	trevally.
aua	yelloweye mullet (commonly herring).
haku	yellowtail kingfish.
hāpuku	groper.
hokarari	ling.
īnanga	whitebait.
kahawai	kahawai.
kanae	grey mullet.
kōkiri	leatherjacket.
kōkopu	kōkopu.
korowhāwhā	anchovy.
kōura	crayfish.
kumukumu	red gurnard.
kūpae	sprat.
kūparu	john dory.
mako	mako shark.
manga	barracouta.
mangō	shark.
mararī	butterfish.
maroro	flying fish.
mohimohi	pilchard.
moki	blue moki.

ngōiro	conger eel.
ngū	squid.
pākaurua	short-tailed stingray.
para	frostfish.
parāoa	sperm whale.
pātiki	sand flounder.
pātiki rori	common sole.
piharau	lamprey.
rāwaru	blue cod.
taiwharu	gudgeon.
takeke	garfish.
tāmure	snapper.
tarakihi	tarakihi.
taumaka	rockfish.
tawatawa	blue mackerel.
tohorā	southern right whale.
ūpokororo	grayling.
whai	short-tailed stingray.
wheke	octopus.